BATTLEFIELD WALKS IN YORKSHIRE

David Clark

Copyright © David Clark, 2003

All Rights Reserved. No part of this publication may be reproduced, stored in a retrieval system, or transmitted in any form or by any means – electronic, mechanical, photocopying, recording, or otherwise – without prior written permission from the publisher or a licence permitting restricted copying issued by the Copyright Licensing Agency, 90 Tottenham Court Road, London W1P 0LA. This book may not be lent, resold, hired out or otherwise disposed of by trade in any form of binding or cover other than that in which it is published, without the prior consent of the publisher.

Published by Sigma Leisure – an imprint of
Sigma Press, 1 South Oak Lane, Wilmslow, Cheshire SK9 6AR, England.

British Library Cataloguing in Publication Data
A CIP record for this book is available from the British Library.

ISBN: 1-85058-775-2

Typesetting and Design by: Sigma Press, Wilmslow, Cheshire.

Cover design: Design House, Marple Bridge
Cover photograph: Battle re-enactment at Ripley, Yorkshire *(Swift Imagery)*

Maps: Bute Cartographics
Photographs: the author

Printed by: MFP Design and Print

Disclaimer: the information in this book is given in good faith and is believed to be correct at the time of publication. No responsibility is accepted by either the author or publisher for errors or omissions, or for any loss or injury howsoever caused. Only you can judge your own fitness, competence and experience. Do not rely solely on sketch maps for navigation: we strongly recommend the use of appropriate Ordnance Survey (or equivalent) maps.

Preface

More major battles have been fought in Yorkshire than in any other English county. It might be argued that Yorkshire covers a wide area and that it would be unusual if a number of battles had not occurred within its boundaries. Yet, the high incidence of military activity does reflect a time when the North of England's prominence in affairs of state often rivalled that of the South. Also, the Great North Road runs through Yorkshire and several famous British battles owe their locations to their proximity to this renowned arterial thoroughfare. The battlefields themselves involve major conflicts between Saxon and Viking, the Scottish Wars, the Wars of the Roses, the English Civil War and the Second World War, when Yorkshire airfields played a vital role in taking the war to Nazi Germany.

The battlefields do tend to be grouped together – as against battlefields in other regions, which tend to be more widely dispersed. Thus, for example, it is possible, within the context of an entertaining – and rewarding – short break in the vicinity of York, to explore Fulford, Stamford Bridge, Marston Moor and the Civil War defences of the city itself.

It is intended that the walks will be of interest simply as walks, even if you have no interest in history. Certainly, you will encounter some splendid landscapes. Even the rather crusty industrial prospects of the West and South Ridings have been softened by the modern landscaper's art. However, by walking the ground once trodden by kings and would-be kings, we can also begin to experience more fully a sense of identity with the past. Half-formed images of famous battles that have shaped our yesterdays spring to life as you stand on a hilltop or in broad pastures where crowns were won and lost.

The walks themselves range between 1 mile and 10 miles in length. Some are countryside walks, while others are essentially urban in character. In the interests of being up-to-date, I have recommended Ordnance Survey Explorer maps, although I find them rather cumbersome and prefer the old Pathfinders. For all the walks, I wore ordinary shoes. Refreshment facilities (e.g. inns) exist on or at the beginning/end of all routes. The walks are not timed because walking pace is a matter for personal preference. And, in a world ob sessed by stringent timekeeping, it is a luxury to allow oneself to lose all sense of time in stepping out into an exploration of over 1,000 years of colourful and exciting history.

David Clark

Contents

Walk 1: Battle of Heathfield   1
    AD 633
    Length: 4½ miles. *Easy.*

Walk 2: Battle of Fulford Gate   6
    20 September 1066
    Length: 4 miles. *Easy.*

Walk 3: Battle of Stamford Bridge   10
    25 September 1066
    Length: 2 miles. *Easy.*

Walk 4: Battle of the Standard   16
    22 August 1138
    Length: 4½ miles. *Moderate.*

Walk 5: Battle of Myton   21
    20 September 1319
    Length: 7 miles. *Moderate.*

Walk 6: Battle of Boroughbridge   26
    16 March 1322
    Length: 4 miles. *Easy.*

Walk 7: Battle of Byland Abbey   32
    14 October 1322
    Length: 7 miles. *Strenuous.*

Walk 8: Battle of Bramham   37
    19 February 1408
    Length: 5 miles. *Moderate.*

Walk 9: Battle of Wakefield   42
    30 December 1460
    Length: 3 miles. *Strenuous.*

Walk 10: Battle of Ferrybridge   47
    28 March 1461
    Length: 2½ miles. *Easy.*

Walk 11: Battle of Towton   52
    29 March 1461
    Length: 7 miles. *Moderate.*

Walk 12: Skirmish at Wetherby   58
    30 November 1642
    Length: 1 mile. Easy.

Walk 13: Battle of Tadcaster   63
    7 December 1642
    Length: 2 miles. Moderate.

Walk 14: Sherburn-in-Elmet   68
    16 December 1642
    Length: 3 miles. Moderate.

Walk 15: Adwalton Moor   72
    30 June 1643
    Length: 4 miles. Moderate.

Walk 16: The Siege of Hull   77
    2 September – 12 October, 1643
    Length: 2 miles. Easy.

Walk 17: Battle of Selby   83
    11 April 1644
    Length: 1 mile. Easy.

Walk 18: Siege of York   88
    21 April to 16 July, 1644
    Length: 3½ miles. Strenuous.

Walk 19: Battle of Marston Moor   96
    2 July 1644
    Length: 10 miles. Moderate.

Walk 20: Siege of Scarborough Castle   103
    18 February – 25 July, 1645
    Length: 2 miles. Strenuous.

Walk 21: Siege of Pontefract   109
    3 June, 1648 – 23 March, 1649
    Length: 1½ miles. Strenuous.

Walk 22: RAF Marston Moor   115
    1941-45
    Length: 5 miles. Easy.

Walk 23: RAF Acaster Malbis   121
    1942-45
    Length: 6 miles. Easy.

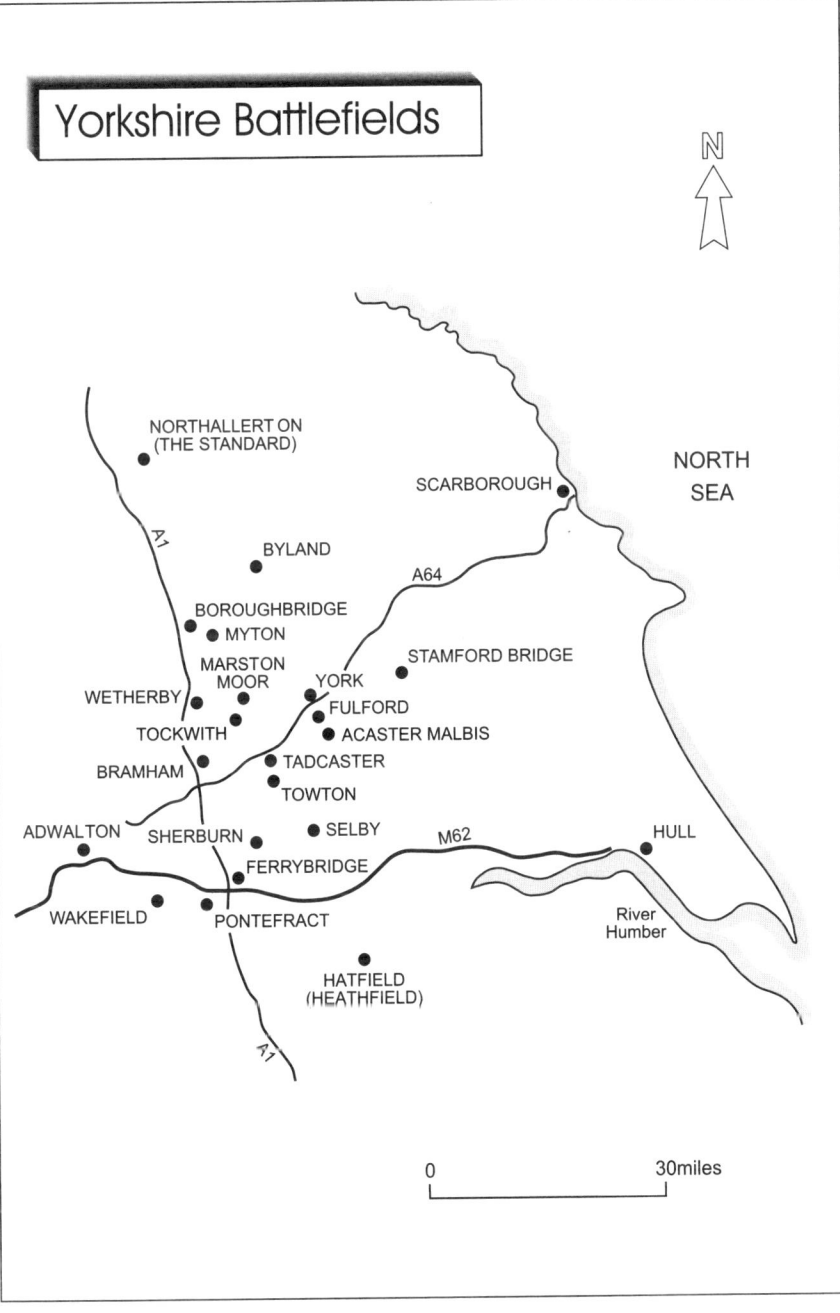

Walk 1: Battle of Heathfield
AD 633

Route: Hatfield – Dunscroft – West End – Hatfield

Starting Point: Hatfield Water Park

Length: 4½ miles. Easy.

Map: Ordnance Survey Explorer 279

Access: Hatfield lies on the A18, 7 miles to the north-east of Doncaster. The Water Park (signposted) is at the eastern end of the village, close to the M18 underpass.

About the Walk

In the 7th century, the greater part of northern Britain, from the River Humber to the Firth of Forth, formed the Kingdom of Northumbria. From AD616, it was ruled by King Edwin who, for the first time, succeeded in uniting much of the country. Bede, in his *History of the English Church and People*, describes Edwin as more powerful than any earlier English king. Edwin is also noteworthy for his conversion to Christianity. This came about because he was keen to cement relations with the Kingdom of Kent. To this end, he married Ethelberga, daughter of Ethelbert, King of Kent. The girl was a Christian and, in order to secure her family's agreement to the contract, Edwin promised that she would have freedom to practise her faith. At length, owing to the influence of his wife and her spiritual advisers, Edwin was converted, along with the Northumbrian nobility and common people.

Edwin's territorial interests extended far to the west, to the isolated Celtic kingdoms of the Isle of Man and Anglesey, both of which he annexed. In addition, he invaded North Wales, incurring the bitter enmity of King Cadwallo. In AD632, Cadwallo – a Briton – formed an alliance with Penda, an ambitious nobleman of Mercia. Together, they aimed to break the power of Northumbria. As their army advanced on Northumbria, Edwin hastily gathered what forces he could and marched out to meet them.

Various locations for the encounter have been suggested, on the grounds that 'Hatfield' constituted a wide administrative area. However, it is popularly believed that the two armies met on or about 12 October AD633 to the north-east of Doncaster, near Hatfield village. Little is known about the course of the battle, but it would have been an essentially primitive affair. At that time, military strategy revolved around the advantages conferred by hilltop positions. High ground could be defended and it could also serve as a platform from which to launch a determined assault on an enemy below. In this flat, marshy landscape, however, high ground was lacking.

St Lawrence's Church in Hatfield was mentioned in the Domesday Book, although the present building dates from the 12th century. For many years, it housed relics from the Battle of Heathfield, which have now been moved to the Royal Armouries in Leeds.

Unbridled savagery also constituted an undeniable tactical advantage, in terms of striking fear into the hearts of one's enemies. The best defence against barbarian savagery was iron discipline, such as that displayed by the Roman legions. In Edwin's case, one wonders whether his conversion to Christianity had dampened his fighting spirit. Certainly, the Battle of Heathfield was over very quickly, and Edwin must have been killed at an early stage. It is said that one of his sons, Osfrid – described by Bede as a gallant young warrior – fell before him. Enraged, Edwin plunged into the thick of the fighting and was himself cut down, together with his ally,

Godbold, King of the Orkneys. In the absence of leadership, Northumbrian resistance collapsed and the entire army was surrounded and destroyed. The result for Britain was catastrophic. Cadwallo embarked on a brutal orgy of ethnic cleansing, designed to exterminate the Anglo-Saxon race. He exhibited Edwin's head on the ramparts of York, thereby establishing a ghastly practice, which would continue for the next thousand years.

The Walk

1. Begin at Hatfield Water Park. From the car park, walk to the main entrance, emerging on to Old Thorne Road, opposite the garage. Turn to the right and walk down to Epworth Road. Turn right to walk into Hatfield. (Call at the Public Library on the left-hand side to pick up a 'town trail' leaflet.)

2. At the T-Junction, turn to the right to see Saint Lawrence's Church – open 2.00-4.00pm Wednesday, Saturday and Sunday. Saint Lawrence's used to contain some relics of the battle, but these are now in the possession of the Royal Armouries in Leeds. This is just as well for, sad to say, the theft of battlefield relics from churches is a not-infrequent occurrence. After viewing the church, follow Manor Road round to Lings Lane, via the footpath on the right-hand side of the road. This is the core of old Hatfield. The area on your right is Dunscroft, a mining town developed in the early 20th century. To your left, the land is still largely undeveloped.

3. At the point where Manor Road becomes Doncaster Road, turn left down Lings Lane. According to tradition, the dead of the Battle of Heathfield were buried here in pits. Walk down Lings Lane to the remains of the windmill. Old maps of the area mark the location of the battle as the fields to the right, suggesting a scenario in which Edwin's men were pressed back and slaughtered to be buried where they fell, at the supposed site of the burial pits.

4. At the end of Lings Lane, after viewing the battlefield from its

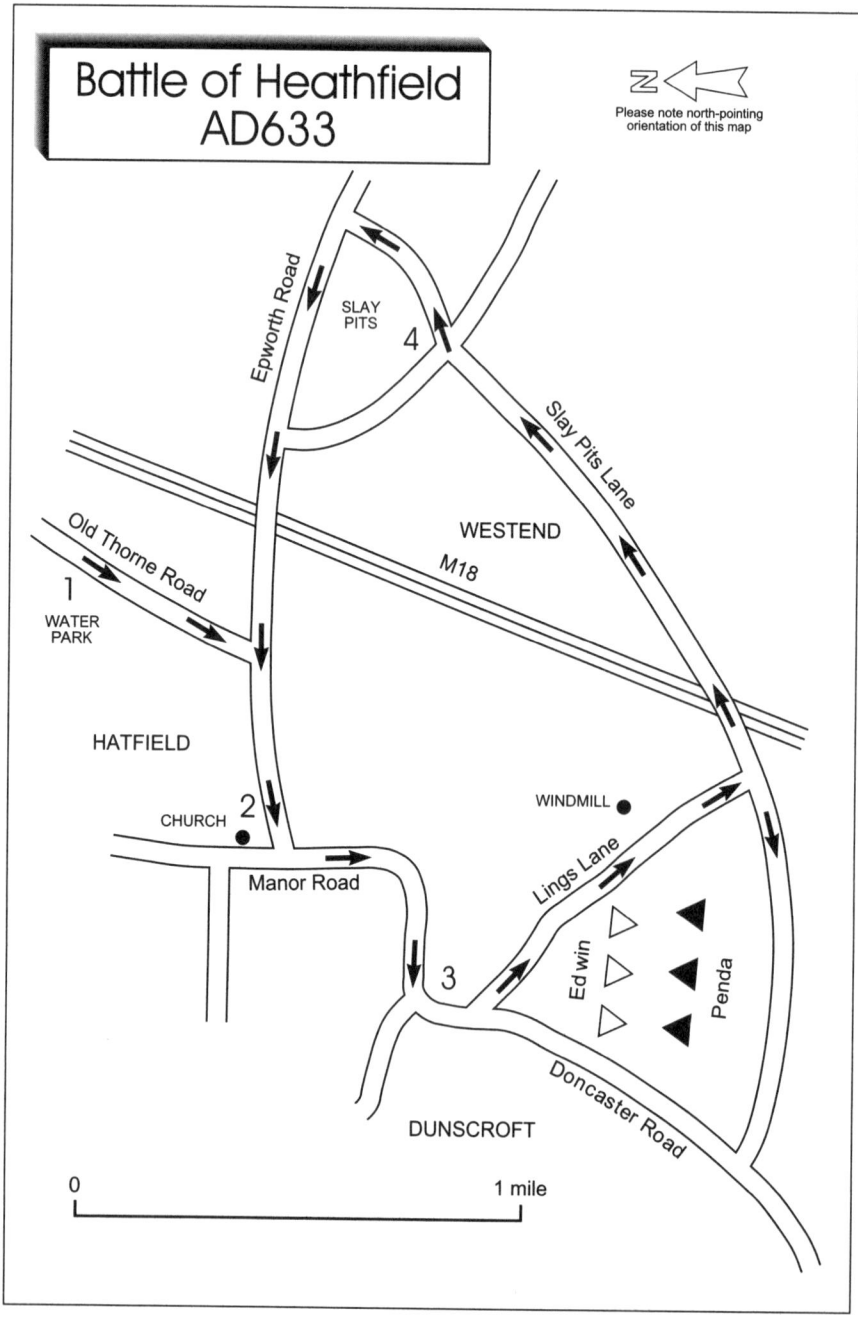

southern end, turn to the left and walk across the M 18 overpass. Continue through West End along a road known as Slay Pits Lane. At the Hatfield Woodhouse junction, take the minor road straight ahead, leading to Slay Pits Farm and Slay Pits – the names suggesting either an alternative location for the Battle of Heathfield or the existence of another earlier battle. At the junction with Epworth Road, turn to the left and walk back over the M18. Old Thorne Road, leading back to the Water Park and your starting point is on your right.

Walk 2: Battle of Fulford Gate
20 September 1066
Route: York – Fulford – York

Starting Point: Fishergate Bar, York

Length: 4 miles. Easy.

Maps: Ordnance Survey Explorer 290/York Street Plan

Access: York can be approached from the A1 on either the A64 or the A59. Use City Centre car parks.

About the Walk

Between 1042 and 1066, England was ruled by Edward the Confessor. His final act before his death in Westminster Abbey was to nominate Harold, Earl of East Anglia and Wessex as his successor. Edward also prophesied that evil would soon fall upon the land, and people scanned the heavens in search of a sign which might be interpreted as God's seal of approval or disapproval on the choice of Harold as sovereign. The omen appeared shortly after Easter 1066, with the arrival of Halley's Comet. A fiery sword, blazing defiantly in the firmament, its appearance was widely accepted as an indication of divine displeasure at Harold's appropriation of the crown.

For some months, Harold's estranged brother, Tostig, had been living in exile in Flanders, where he passed his time plotting Harold's downfall. Seeking help, he approached William, Duke of Normandy, only to find that William had plans of his own. He was more fortunate in his overtures to the King of Norway, Harold Hardrada, who agreed to help Tostig challenge his brother's supremacy. Hardrada amassed an invasion force of 9,000 men, comprising Norwegians, Scots and Tostig's own followers. Setting sail from the Orkney Islands – dependencies of Norway – towards the end of August 1066, this formidable force wrought havoc along the north-east coastline of Britain before turning in to the River Humber. Pressing on into the River Ouse, the fleet finally came to rest at Riccall.

Walk 2: Battle of Fulford Gate

Battlefield exploration should always take account of an army's preliminary manoeuvres. In the cases of Fulford and Stamford Bridge, a visit to Riccall Landing (7 miles to the south of York/OS Explorer 290 6037), location of Hadrada's base camp, is of interest. A feature of the approach, along Landing Lane is the 'Old Riccall Mill Restaurant' – an intriguing and tasteful adaption of a 19th-century tower mill.

King Harold had been expecting an invasion from Normandy, led by William. To meet this challenge, he was camped with his army on the Isle of Wight. It was left to others, therefore, to do whatever they could to stop Hardrada's rampaging hordes.

On 20 September, Hardrada left his fleet at Riccall, 10 miles to the south of York and marched on the city. Resistance was co-ordinated by Morcar, Earl of Northumbria and his brother Edwin, Earl of Mercia. Together, they gathered a substantial force, which they marched, along the banks of the River Ouse, to Fulford, a settlement between York and Riccall.

Here, they met Hardrada who deployed his men along a line which stretched from the Ouse inland, towards a dyke, beyond which was a deep and wide swamp. His forces were thickest by the river, while the line by the dyke was clearly thinner and weaker. Earl Morcar led his men in close formation along the river bank and, perceiving the apparent weakness on Hardrada's right wing, directed his attack towards it. The right wing gave way, with the English in pursuit. In fact, Morcar had been caught by the oldest of Viking tricks. As soon as the English had been drawn in, Hardrada sprung his trap and wheeled round his left wing to trap them against the dyke and the swamp. So unexpected and so fierce was the onslaught that the English force was destroyed. Those who were not cut down by the invaders were pushed back over the dyke to find a watery grave in the swamp.

Hardrada's peace terms were surprisingly generous. In exchange for hostages and supplies, York – the third most important city in the country – would not be sacked. The citizens agreed to meet the Norwegians on 25 September, when hostages and provisions would be handed over. The chosen meeting place was eight miles to the east of York at a spot on the River Derwent called Stamford Bridge.

The Walk

1. Begin in Fishergate in York. Walk down Fishergate towards Fulford Road – the A19. Turn into New Walk Terrace on your right, which leads on to a riverside path, New Walk – now part of the long-distance footpath, 'Minster Way'. You are now following the route taken by the Saxon army marching out from York – and the route taken by the fleeing survivors after the battle.

2. At St Oswald's Church at the end of St Oswald's Road, New Walk becomes Love Lane. Continue along Love Lane, which gradually veers away from the River Ouse. This portion of the walk was probably the scene of heavy fighting as the Norwegians succeeded in turning the Saxon left wing.

3. Continue walking to the end of Love Lane, bearing right then left to walk along the path hugging the river bank. Turn left into Landing Lane and left again on to Main Street. Take the next right turn into Fordlands Road, bearing left into Fulford Mews, which leads on to the track known as Germany Lane. Imagine a dyke against which much of the Saxon army was pressed – eventually spilling over into the swamp which, at that time, comprised the landscape.

4. Retrace your steps to Main Street, turning right, and continue into Fulford Road which can be followed back to your starting point in Fishergate – a route which takes you past the army barracks, where soldiers have been billeted since 1795.

Walk 2: Battle of Fulford Gate

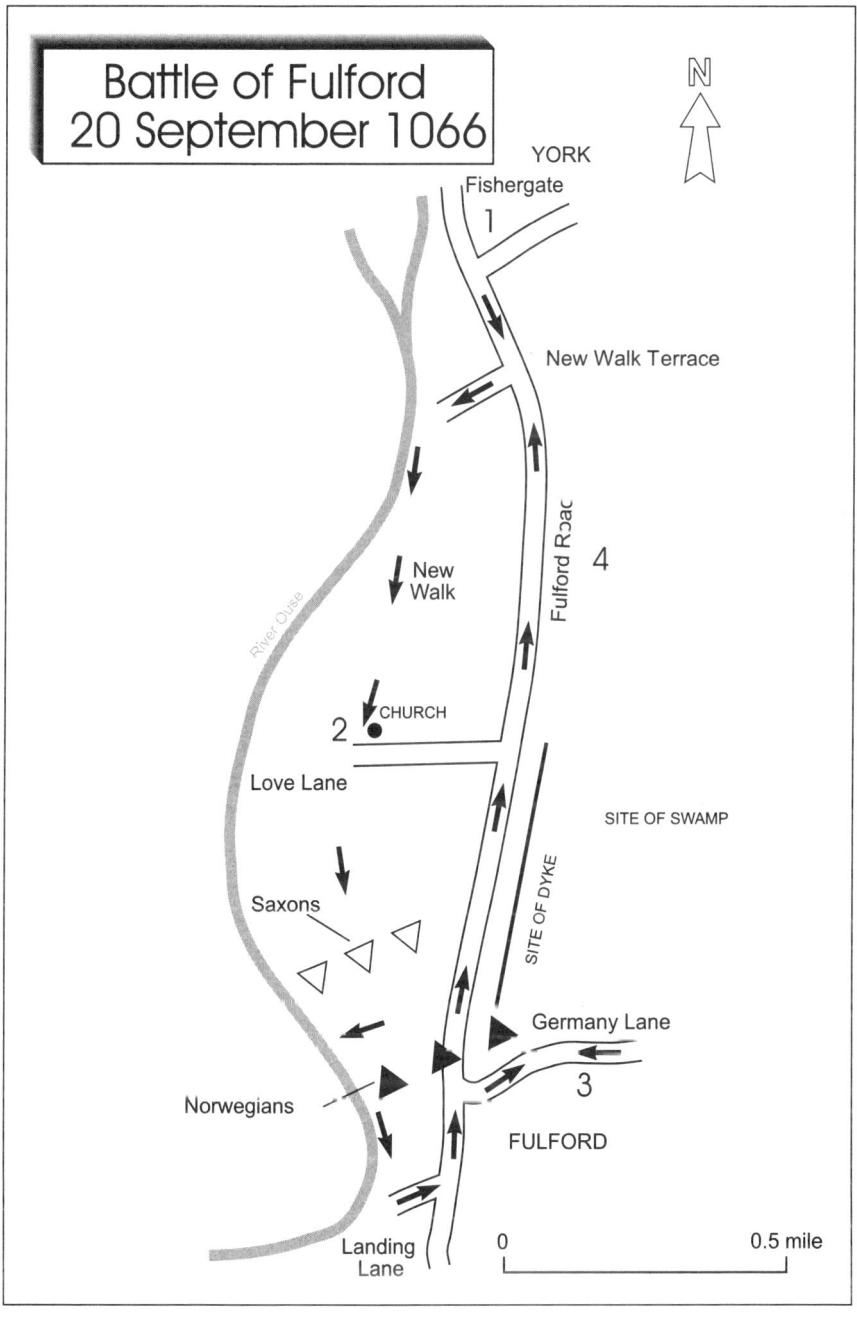

Walk 3: Battle of Stamford Bridge

25 September 1066

Route: Stamford Bridge – Battle Flats – Stamford Bridge

Starting Point: Picnic site (with car parking) on the south side of the bridge.

Length: 2 miles. Easy.

Map: Ordnance Survey Explorer 294

Access: Stamford Bridge lies on the A166, 7 miles to the east of York and, with York encircled by a ring road, is easily accessible from all directions. (During the summer months. delays can occur at the bridge, which is restricted to one-way traffic controlled by traffic lights.)

About the Walk

After their success at the Battle of Fulford on 20 September 1066, the Norwegian invaders of England, under their leader, Harold Hardrada, accepted the submission of the citizens of York who, by their capitulation, hoped to be spared. It is likely that Tostig – estranged brother of the English king, Harold – anxious to secure their future loyalty, saved them from destruction. Hardrada was to be furnished with provisions and given the sons of the leading citizens to hold as hostages. It was agreed that a meeting would subsequently be held at Stamford Bridge, where homage would be paid to Hardrada, who would appoint officials to rule York and distribute titles and estates. Additional hostages from the county were to be provided and, to this end, Stamford Bridge was a good choice of location. In addition to a bridge linking the east and west banks of the River Derwent, all the major roads in that part of Yorkshire converged here. Accordingly, on 24 September, Hardrada set out for Stamford Bridge, leaving one third of his force at Riccall to guard his boats. What he did not know was that on the same day, King Harold was at Tadcaster, having just completed one of the most famous forced marches of all time. He had covered almost 200 miles in five

Walk 3: Battle of Stamford Bridge

The 'Swordsman Inn', Stamford Bridge – one of several inviting watering places in the village – is named after the Norwegian stalwart who held the bridge against all comers.

days, marching from the Isle of Wight, where he had been awaiting an invasion by William of Normandy. In the early hours of 25 September, Harold entered York, where he was appraised of the situation. Almost immediately, he struck out for Stamford Bridge where Hardrada was waiting confidently for tribute.

Perhaps the Norwegians did not anticipate Harold's approach from the west. It may be that they did not expect him at all, but the rapid approach of the English later in the morning of 25 September caught them at a disadvantage on the west bank of the Derwent. Hardrada withdrew most of his men to a ridge on the Derwent's east bank, leaving a smaller body of troops on the bridge to cover his retreat. No sooner had the English arrived than they bore down upon the bridge, a modest wooden structure, so narrow that it could be used by only one or two men at a time. The Norwegian rearguard was swamped by sheer weight of numbers. Finally, there remained only one defender on the bridge itself – a gigantic fellow armed with a double-headed axe – who defied all efforts to dislodge him. He was removed only by a subterfuge. An English soldier managed to acquire a swill-tub (a trough for feeding hogs), using it to float under the bridge and despatch the worthy Horatius with an upward spear thrust.

Hardrada had deployed his main body of troops in an area subsequently known as Battle Flats. They were drawn up in a horseshoe formation with Hardrada and Tostig, each with his personal retinue, occupying the centre. Harold launched his men at the defensive wall of shields. This was to be no replay of the Battle of Fulford, for Harold's house-carls – well-equipped, disciplined, highly trained professionals – were more than a match for the enemy. It was all the Norwegians could do to hold their ground as, inch by inch, the house-carls, with Harold at their head, pressed forward. Gradually, an increasing number of gaps appeared in the Norwegian defences, and the concentrated fighting broke up into a series of small group and individual combats.

With an occasional lull, this bruising contest went on for the better part of the day until men on both sides were dropping from sheer exhaustion. An input of fresh troops would have proved decisive. Harold had no hopes of such reinforcements, but the Norwegians had summoned aid from their base camp at Riccall. Unfortunately, the Norwegian reserves were so fatigued when they did arrive that they threw off their chain mail, and so fell easy prey to sword and axe. Although the tide of battle did turn briefly in favour of the invaders, the English held on. At last, Hardrada was felled by one of the few English archers on the field, while a house-carl's axe split Tostig's skull down to the jaw bone. With the death of their leaders, the Norwegians' resistance collapsed. Despite their own weariness, the victors began a long and bloody pursuit of the enemy, now fleeing in panic to the temporary safety of their fleet.

For Harold, it was a stunning victory. Taking into account Fulford, Stamford Bridge and the slaughter which followed, upwards of 5,000 of the invaders perished on English soil. Whereas the invasion force had required 300 troop ships, only 24 were needed to ferry home the survivors. The remainder of the once-proud Armada was put to the torch. Of the enemy dead, those of exalted rank received decent burials, while the bodies of the common soldiers were left to rot where they lay. Yet, Harold's victory celebrations were short-lived, for even as he made his triumphant entry into York, William, Duke of Normandy, was making final preparations for his own invasion of England.

The Walk

1. Begin at the picnic site on the south side of the present-day bridge. From here, cross The Square to the village green to view a display board containing a descriptive battle plan. Next to the green is The Shallows section of the River Derwent. In all probability, the river would have been fordable over The Shallows and the wooden bridge of the battle would have been adjacent to it.

2. Return to the road and walk up Main Street. On a mound opposite the Bay Horse Inn, there is a stone memorial bearing an inscription advising us that the battle was 'fought in this neighbourhood'. Continue walking along Main Street, out of the village and on to the A166 Driffield road.

3. On the right-hand side of the road is a modern housing estate. Built squarely across the battlefield, the development has not added to the ambience of this important historical site. At the end of the estate is a footpath, which develops into a farm track leading into what was probably an area of heavy fighting.

4. Where the track veers to the left, pause for a moment. Ahead, the land rises towards the Yorkshire Wolds. The Norwegians may have felt that the gentle gradient would give them an edge against Harold's men, marching up from the river. To the right is the undulating country across which the weary Norwegian relief column would have struggled in their dash from Riccall. Down through the centuries, swords, spears and horseshoes have been unearthed on this land, just as fragments of weaponry have been recovered from the Derwent.

5. In 1958, on my first visit to Stamford Bridge, it was possible to walk across the battlefield via a public footpath which has long since disappeared. An alternative route, intended to replace the

14 *Battlefield Walks in Yorkshire*

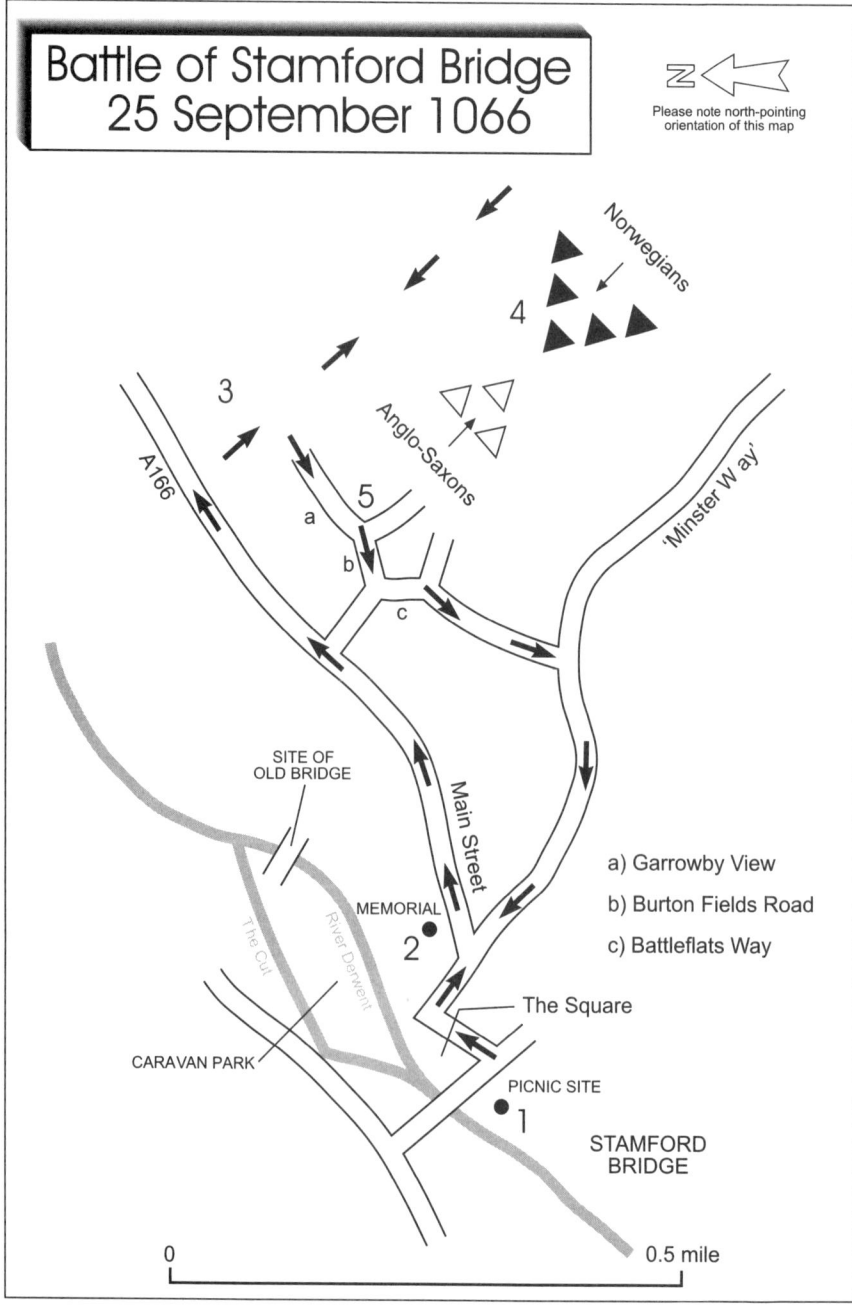

original, has fallen into disuse and it is necessary, therefore, to retrace your steps to the housing estate. Instead of returning to the A166, however, turn left into the housing estate at Garrowby View. Turn right into Burton Fields Road and then bear left into Battleflats Way. This road eventually links up with the Wilberfoss road.

6. By turning left into the Wilberfoss road – part of the long distance footpath, 'Minster Way', running between York and Beverley, you are able to view the Battle Flats area from the south east. Retrace your steps and follow the road back into the village and your starting point at the picnic area.

Walk 4: Battle of the Standard
22 August 1138

Route: Brompton – Standard Hill – Oaktree Hill – Brompton

Starting point: Northallerton Road, Brompton

Length: 4½ miles. Moderate.

Map: Ordnance Survey Explorer 302

Access: The battlefield lies about three miles to the north of Northallerton, on the A167 Northallerton-Darlington road. Parking available in Brompton.

About the Walk

When Henry I died in 1135, the English crown was seized by his nephew, Stephen of Blois. Although Henry's daughter, Matilda, was Henry's legitimate heir – and his preferred choice – it was thought inappropriate for a woman to occupy such an elevated position and Stephen attracted the necessary baronial support. Matilda refused to relinquish her claim and was encouraged by the Scottish king, David I. His support for her cause provided him with an excuse for mounting border raids, which became bywords for brutality and savagery.

At length, in the summer of 1138, David crossed the border at Carlisle, at the head of an army of 12,000 men – a mongrel host comprising Scots, disaffected English, Norwegians, Normans, Germans and Danes. Stephen, preoccupied with baronial rebellions in the south, was in no position to address the problem and David was able to ravage Northumberland unmolested before pressing on into North Yorkshire. English resistance was co-ordinated by Archbishop Thurstan of York, who also held the office of Lieutenant of the North. Thurstan cobbled together a scratch army which proceeded to Thirsk where attempts to appease the Scots failed. The two armies continued to advance until they met on gently rising ground three miles to the north of Northallerton.

Here, at dawn on 22 August, was raised the English 'standard' from which the coming battle took its name. A curious contraption, it consisted of a ship's mast fixed to a cart. On top of the mast, a consecrated wafer was enclosed in a pyx (a vessel more usually found in a church). From cross-pieces nailed to the mast lower down were hanging the sacred banners of St Peter of York, St John of Beverley, St Wilfred of Ripon and St Cuthbert of Durham. While it also served to symbolise the crusading nature of the enterprise, its primary purpose was to act as a rallying point for the English army.

The recently renovated roadside monument to the 'Battle of The Standard' depicts the English standard – a mast affixed to a low, four-wheeled carriage.

Detailed accounts of the troop formations vary, but it is probable that the English lines followed the traditional deployment of archers to the fore, spearmen directly behind and knights in the rear. David, on the other hand, was hamstrung by a contingent of wild Galwegian (Men of Galloway) tribesmen who insisted on fighting in the front line.

Battle commenced with a ferocious Galwegian charge, which was halted in its tracks by murderous volleys of English arrows. The Galwegian leader – the Earl of Lothian – and two chieftains, Ulgeric and Dunewald, were among the casualties. Leaderless, the men of Galloway recoiled, falling back on their own lines. As often happened in such situations, they found their path blocked by their own advancing ranks, which heightened the confusion and spread panic.

On the right wing of the Scottish line stood a division of knights, spearmen and archers, commanded by David's son, Prince Henry. Hoping to turn the tide, the Prince led a charge which broke through the English lines. However, the gap he had created was quickly closed behind him, cutting him off from his own side. He could extricate himself only by throwing a cloak over his distinctive armour and mingling with the enemy. By the time he had worked his way back to his own portion of the field, the English had pressed home their initial advantage and the Scottish army was in full retreat.

Both King David and Prince Henry reached Carlisle in safety. The English made no concerted effort to pursue the rank and file, although stragglers were shown no mercy if discovered along the way. Fifty Scottish knights were taken prisoner and held to ransom, while the total number of Scottish dead was said to exceed 10,000. Immediately after its victory, the English army disbanded, leaving the borders undefended and enabling the Scots to continue to raid at will.

The Walk

1. Begin in Brompton by the church, at the corner of Northallerton Road. Walk down Northallerton Road until, past the church on your right, you reach Lodge Lane, leading to Highfield Farm. Walk up Lodge Lane, under the railway line. At the point where the track bears left to the farm, continue straight on, along the public footpath.

2. The footpath hugs the right-hand boundary of the narrow field ahead. It then runs diagonally across the large field ahead of you – aim for the farm (Firtree Farm) buildings. Cross over into the next field and head for the far right-hand corner. A footbridge crosses a stream to your right and the path returns to hugging the field boundary. Bear to the right across a second footbridge and continue straight on to emerge on the A167.

Walk 4: Battle of the Standard   19

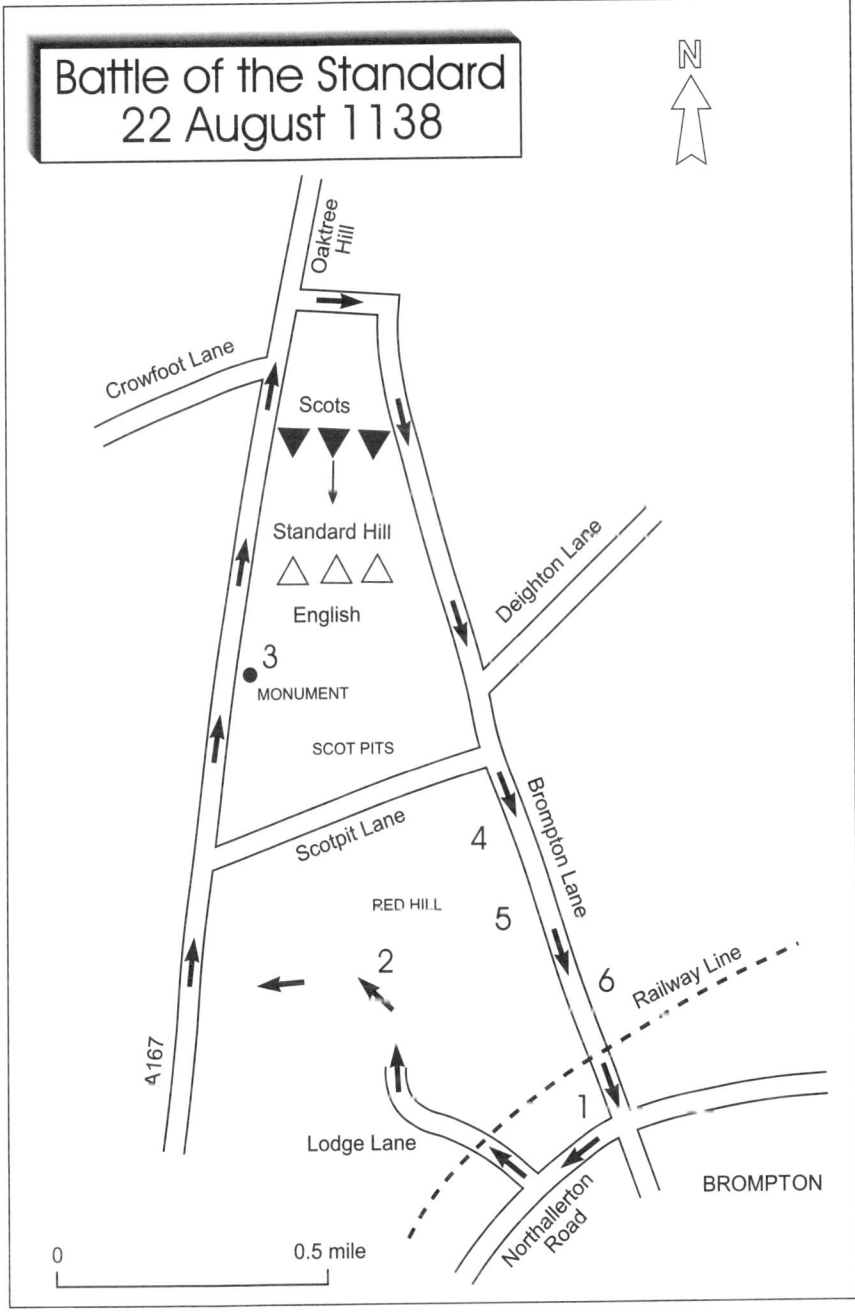

3. Turn right and walk up the A167 until you come to the battlefield monument – a little beyond Cinnamire Farm. The strength of the English position is immediately apparent and it is easy to visualise the front lines strung out across the ridge a little to the north of the monument and down the slope to the road. Proceed northward along the grass verge. To your left is Malt Shovel Farm, beyond which were the Scots. Continue walking as far as the garage and turn right into Brompton Lane.

4. Walk down Brompton Lane. You will have observed that the Scottish position was also strong but, as in many instances in the saga of Anglo-Scottish warfare, the Scots chose to abandon it, to charge downhill and then up to the ridge occupied by the English. Further down the hill, past the junction with Deighton Lane and opposite a cottage, is an overgrown track known as Scotpit Lane. The area immediately in front of it marks the mass graves of the slaughtered Galwegians whose bodies were thrown into burial pits. Fragments of bones and weapons have been found here. Now virtually impassable, the lane is barely recognisable as more than a rough path beaten through the undergrowth – a lonely, cheerless spot. At one time, it connected Brompton Lane with the A167, but its status now is unclear, alternately disappearing and reappearing on successive editions of Ordnance Survey maps.

5. Keep walking and you will reach Red Hill – an alternative suggested location for the battle. In some respects, it is more feasible. Given that the battlefield dead were usually buried where they fell, you can easily envisage a scenario in which the Scots, occupying a position forward of Scotpit Lane, were pressed back and cut down in the vicinity of the Scot Pits.

6. Continue down Brompton Lane and walk under the railway line, after which the road becomes Station Road, running down into Brompton and your starting point at Northallerton Road junction.

Walk 5: Battle of Myton
20 September 1319

Route: Boroughbridge – Milby – Myton-on-Swale – Ellenthorpe – Milby – Boroughbridge

Starting Point: Picnic Area by the roundabout near the bridge (B6265) in Boroughbridge.

Length: 7 miles. Moderate.

Map: Ordnance Survey Explorer 299

Access: Myton-on-Swale is not very accessible by road. Hence, the best starting point is Boroughbridge on the B6265 off the A1, 17 miles to the north west of York.

About the Walk

Edward I reigned from 1272 to 1307. He spent his latter years trying to subjugate Scotland and succeeded to such an extent that he acquired the sobriquet 'The Hammer of the Scots.' His son, Edward II, was sadly lacking in his father's abilities and the Scots soon took advantage of his weakness. Robert the Bruce raided across the border at will. In 1313, he seized the Isle of Man and, one by one, the English strongholds fell: Dundee, Perth, Dumfries. At last, in 1314, in their defence of Stirling, the Scots enjoyed their most famous victory against the English, at Bannockburn. In 1318, the Scots captured Berwick and Edward marched north to lay siege to the garrison.

While Edward was preoccupied with Berwick, a Scottish army of 10,000, led by the Earl of Moray and the Earl of Douglas, crossed into England. The customary orgy of pillage, fire and murder was incidental to a cunning master plan to march on York and capture Isabella, Edward's queen, who was known to be in the city. The plot was discovered and Isabella was removed to the comparative safety of Nottingham, while the Archbishop of York assembled a force to meet the approaching Scots.

Although he managed to amass some 10,000 men, they were

St Mary's Church, Myton. In 1820, the remains of Roger de Mowbray, participant in the Battle of The Standard and founder of Byland Abbey, were removed from the abbey and interred here.

mostly ill-fitted for combat. There were many churchmen – including the Bishop of Ely, the Abbot of Selby, the Abbot of St Mary's at York and the Dean of York – and the Lord Mayor of York, Sir Nicholas Fleming, with as many citizens and peasants who could be pressed into service. They set off from York, following the east bank of the River Swale. They knew where to find the Scots who were camped at the village of Myton, three miles to the east of Boroughbridge – and the Scots knew that they were coming. The Archbishop and his followers had no battle plan, and behaved as though they were about to disperse a band of vagabonds instead of an army of seasoned campaigners. The opposing forces met in the afternoon of 20 September 1319. Just below Myton, the River Swale was spanned by a wooden bridge and the Scots, encamped on the west bank, lured the Archbishop's men across to where they lay in ambush. As soon as the English were across and before they were able to organise themselves, the Scots set fire to three haystacks. The smoke blinded the English who were unable to stop the invaders from cutting off their line of retreat over the bridge. What followed was not so much a battle as a slaughter. The Scots attacked on two fronts and the English, being trapped between the Scots and the Swale were cut down in droves. Three thousand were killed and a further thousand were drowned. Among the dead were over 200 monks clad in white habits – hence the alternative name for the encounter: White Battle. But for the onset of darkness, many more would have died. Most of the leaders – except Sir Nicholas Fleming – being possessed of swift horses, managed to escape.

The Walk

1. Begin at the Picnic Site at the roundabout by the bridge in Boroughbridge. At the roundabout, walk up the minor road to Milby. Walk through the hamlet and turn to the right at the junction.

2. Walk up Ellenthorpe Lane to Clot House Farm, beyond which the track becomes a bridleway. When you cross Myton Pasture Stell, you are in Myton Pasture – the site of the battle.

3. Follow the bridleway which skirts the trees before turning sharp right at the field boundary ahead. This leads directly to Myton Bridge. This structure replaced the original bridge, which was destroyed by fire. Cross the bridge and walk into the village.

4. Walk up to the church where some of the dead – doubtless the ecclesiastics – were buried in the churchyard. Some of the stones from the original bridge were incorporated into the fabric of the church itself.

5. Retrace your steps to the bridge. The Scots were camped in Myton Pasture, before you, while the English advanced along the east bank of the Swale. Cross over and take the riverside path to your left. The original bridge stood about 200 yards downriver. Continue walking, with the trees on your right, crossing Myton Pasture Stell and walking down to the confluence of the Swale and the Ure. Cut off from retreat across the bridge, it was into this trap that the English army was herded.

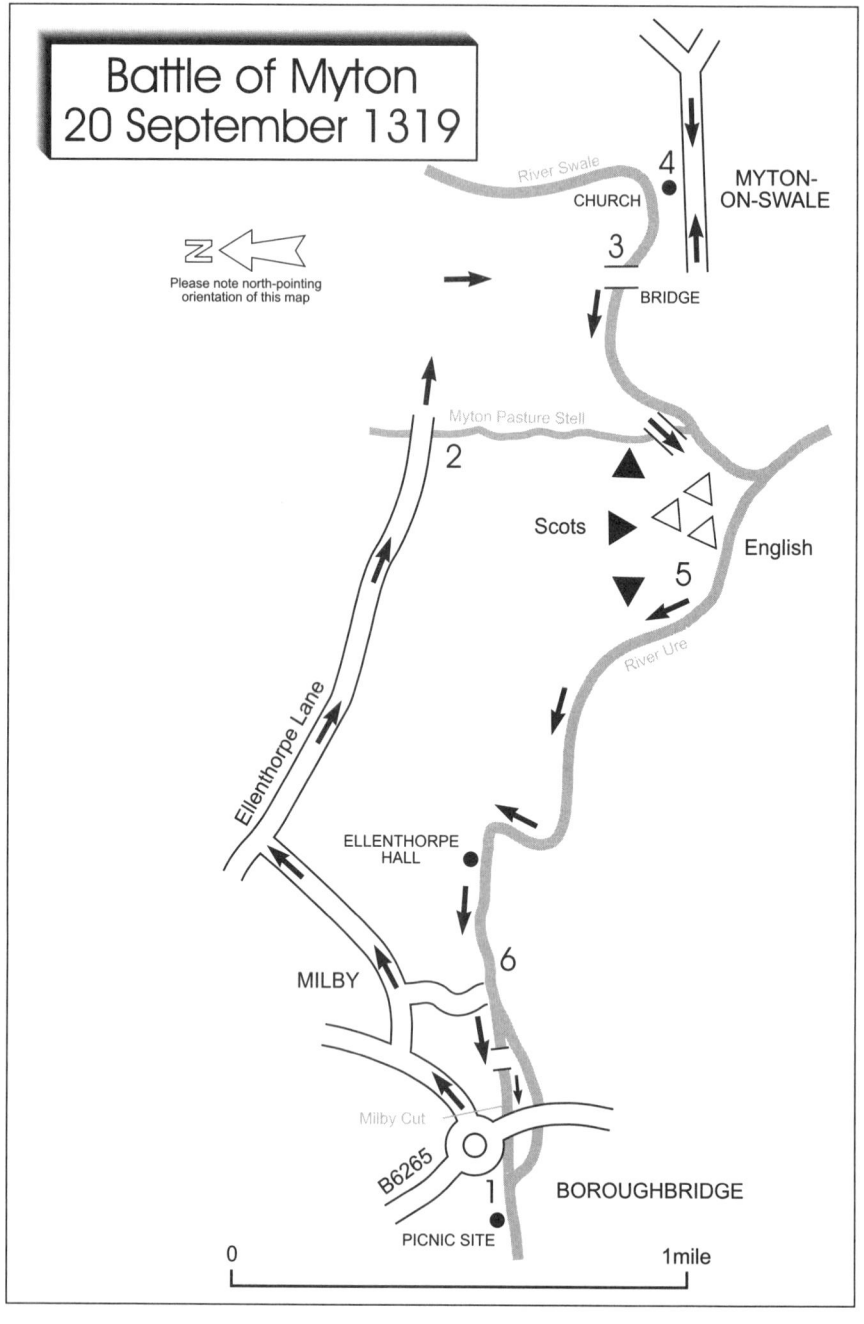

6. Follow the riverside path up to Ellenthorpe Hall, where the path veers away from the river for a short distance before rejoining it. Bear to the left until you come to Milby Cut. The landing here is of interest because it was the scene of fighting during the Earl of Lancaster's rebellion of 1322 – see Walk 6: The Battle of Boroughbridge. Continue walking and cross the footbridge over Milby Cut. Once over the bridge, bear to the right to emerge at the roundabout.

Note: repairs to Myton Bridge are expected to be completed in December 2002.

Walk 6: Battle of Boroughbridge

16 March 1322

Route: Boroughbridge – Aldborough – Boroughbridge

Starting point: Picnic Site at the roundabout on the north bank of the River Ure

Length: 4 miles. Easy.

Map: Ordnance Survey Explorer 299

Access: Boroughbridge is located on the B6265, off the A1, 17 miles to the north west of York. Parking is available at the Picnic Site.

About the Walk

The campaigns of King Edward II against the Scots fell somewhat short of the standards set by his father, Edward I. In 1314, there was the unmitigated disaster of Bannockburn, and in 1319, the fruitless siege of Berwick, which led, indirectly, to the Battle of Myton. Although his father's exploits in Scotland had been famous, they had also been partly responsible for saddling his successor with a national debt of £200,000 – no mean sum for the time. Savings had to be made, and so the Scottish problem was put on the back burner – which offended the northern barons who felt they were being abandoned to the depredations of Scottish raiding parties.

As if this were not enough, Edward also had pressing domestic problems. He had lost much initial goodwill through his infatuation with his male lover, Piers Gaveston. When Gaveston was murdered, Edward replaced him with another favourite, Hugh Despenser, who amassed a personal fortune of a magnitude which defies description. Not unnaturally, this brought the king into conflict with some of his most powerful barons. Cleverly, Edward picked them off one by one until those still at large – the Earl of Lancaster, Hugh Audley the Younger, Sir Roger Clifford and the Earl of Hereford – and their modest rebel army were being hunted by Royal forces commanded by the Earls of Surrey and Kent.

Walk 6: Battle of Boroughbridge

The Battle Cross, 14th century in origin, is said to commemorate the Battle of Boroughbridge. Removed to its present site in nearby Aldborough in 1852, it was restored in 1967 by the Aldborough and Boroughbridge Preservation Society.

Lancaster and his supporters managed to elude their pursuers and gain the security of Lancaster's own stronghold of Pontefract Castle, which he considered capable of withstanding a protracted siege. However, his allies insisted on moving north, to make a stand at the impregnable Dunstanburgh Castle in Northumberland. Bowing to this pressure, a disheartened Lancaster set out for Dunstanburgh on a route that took the rebels via Boroughbridge, where they arrived on 16 March 1322, in the expectation of passing the night in safety.

Lancaster's scouting arrangements must have left much to be desired, for after his army had begun to settle in, he learned that the bridge over the River Ure at the north end of the town was already in the hands of Sir Andrew de Harcla, Warden of Carlisle and the Western Marches, acting for the king. Lancaster tried to parlay with de Harcla, reminding him of past favours – de Harcla had received his knighthood from the Earl – but de Harcla would have none of it. Although his own force was numerically inferior, he knew that the narrow rickety bridge would not be an easy objective. Additionally, he could eventually expect the arrival of the main Royal army.

When it was clear that de Harcla could not be bought off, battle commenced. At first, activity was limited to volleys of arrows, which the archers of each side projected across the river. As the rebels could not afford to become pinned down, however, the Earl of Hereford led a direct assault on the bridge while Lancaster, commanding a party of horse, tried to outflank de Harcla by crossing the river by a ford, further downstream, at Milby. To Lancaster's dismay, he found the ford well guarded by a company of archers, and he was forced to retire. At the bridge, Hereford's contingent made good progress before the Earl himself was despatched by a Welsh spearman who, having climbed beneath the bridge, disembowelled him with an upward thrust of his spear. This episode, as recounted by contemporary chroniclers, may have owed something to the account of the courageous Norwegian's death at the Battle of Stamford Bridge. Whatever the cause of Hereford's demise, it had the effect of spreading panic among the rebels. When Clifford was felled by an arrow, the offensive broke down completely and the rebels retreated in disorder.

Aware of the fact that the battle was lost, Lancaster concluded a temporary truce with de Harcla, by which he agreed to surrender on the following morning, or suffer the consequences. This led to the extraordinary situation of the vanquished retiring into Boroughbridge to sleep soundly, while the victors remained on stand-by through the night, continuing to guard both the bridge and the ford. It may have been that de Harcla, mindful of his debt to Lancaster, wanted to give him an opportunity to slip away, but dawn saw the arrival of the High Sheriff of Yorkshire with royal reinforcements and de Harcla was compelled to attack the town.

Abandoned by all save a faithful few, Lancaster tried to claim sanctuary in the chapel in the market square. Dragged from the altar, he was stripped of his armour and forced to wear his servant's clothing. Later, he was shipped to York where he was pelted with mud by the citizens – the same folk who would gladly have adorned him with garlands, had his revolt been successful. On 22 March 1322, he was beheaded on a hill close to his own Pontefract Castle.

The Walk

1. Begin at the Picnic Site by the roundabout on the north bank of the River Ure. This location provides a good view of the present-day bridge from upstream. The land on this side of the river rises gently to overlook the opposite bank, providing a good vantage point for de Harcla's archers. Below the bridge, remnants of armour, helmets, axe-heads and other arms have, from time to time, been discovered.

2. Cross over the bridge into Horsefair and continue down to Bar Lane on the right. Make a detour along Bar Lane where, towards the end – just before the A1 overpass – can be found the Devil's Arrows, three standing stones. Two stand in the field to the right and one of them is hidden in the trees to the left. Three thousand years ago, they were hauled laboriously – each weighs 30 tons – over six miles from Knaresborough. Originally, there were four but one was torn down and used to build a bridge over the River Tutt, the Ure's tributary running through the town. They may have played a role in fertility rites but, whatever their purpose, one cannot help wondering what effect their presence would have had upon the superstitious minds of the combatants of the battle.

3. Walk back up to Horsefair, bearing left and then right into St Helena, which leads on to Aldborough Road. Opposite the school, take the public footpath leading to the River Ure. Lancaster would have crossed these open fields to reach the ford at Milby.

4. At the Ure, turn to the right along the raised riverside path which follows the south bank of the river. The ford itself lies beyond the lock and, as at the bridge, the north bank commands a clear view of the land to the south, which helped de Harcla's archers keep the rebels at bay. Continue along the path to Hall Arm Lane, which runs by the side of Aldborough Hall into the village of Aldborough. Bear right into the village and walk to the 14th-century St Andrew's Church. Aldborough, originally called Iseur, was the Brigante tribal capital. Under the Roman occupa-

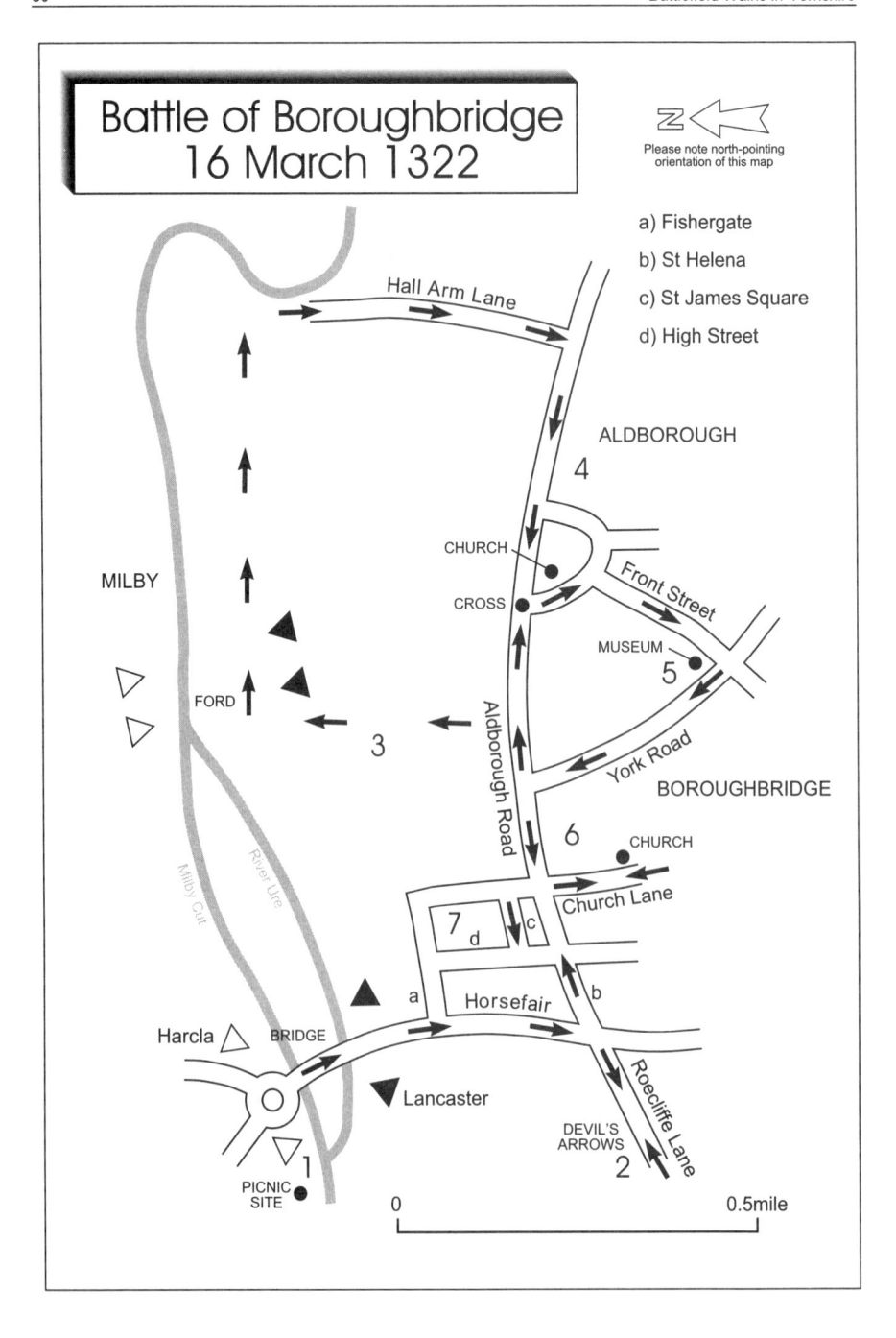

Battle of Boroughbridge
16 March 1322

Please note north-pointing orientation of this map

a) Fishergate
b) St Helena
c) St James Square
d) High Street

tion, it became Isurium Brigantum. Stone from some of the Roman buildings was used in the construction of the church tower and the church itself contains a statue of the Roman god, Mercury. A few yards further along the road is the Battle Cross, commemorating the Battle of Boroughbridge. Erected shortly after the battle, it stood in the market place in Boroughbridge for 500 years until 1852 when it was removed to its present site.

5. At the cross, a left turn will take you down to Front Street, the main thoroughfare of the Roman settlement. At the end of the road is an English Heritage museum displaying local Roman finds.

6. From the museum, turn right into York Road, which leads back to Boroughbridge. At the end, turn left into Aldborough Road and left again into Church Lane to see St James's Church. The chapel in which the wretched Lancaster sought sanctuary stood in St James's Square. It was pulled down in 1851 to facilitate the exploitation of an artesian well. The present-day church contains fragments of carved stone belonging to the chapel, depicting, in particular, two representations of the Crucifixion – perhaps the very carvings before which Lancaster knelt in despair.

7. Walk back up Church Lane and across St James's Square into High Street, on into Fishergate and back over the bridge to your starting point at the Picnic Site.

Walk 7: Battle of Byland Abbey
14 October 1322

Route: Byland Abbey – Oldstead – Byland Abbey

Starting Point: Byland Abbey. Parking available.

Length: 7 miles. Strenuous.

Maps: Ordnance Survey Explorer 299 & 300

Access: Byland Abbey lies within the North Yorkshire Moors National Park, 2 miles to the south of the A170 Scarborough-Thirsk road. It can also be approached via the A19 Thirsk-Darlington road or the A64 York-Scarborough road.

About the Walk

No sooner had King Edward II dealt with the rebel barons who opposed his rule at the Battle of Boroughbridge than the Scots once more demanded his attention. The increasing severity of border raids – particularly in Cumberland – could not go unchallenged. Parliament voted the money and an English army of between 60,000 and 100,000 men, including a strong contingent of foreign mercenaries, was raised. Yet, even as preparations were taking place, Robert the Bruce was pillaging at will. On an extended tour of between three and four weeks, he devastated much of Cumberland and even a portion of Lancashire, finally returning to Scotland laden with booty and captives.

Towards the end of July 1322, Edward despatched his fleet to the Firth of Forth, and on 1 August, he set out for Scotland with his army. As he crossed the border, the Scots retired before him. Their retreat was tactical for, by pursuing a scorched earth policy, they ensured that no supplies fell into English hands. Edward had experienced logistical problems eight years before, during the Bannockburn campaign, but it seems that he had failed to learn the lesson. As he advanced, unopposed, towards Edinburgh, his men became weak from hunger. Disease – notably dysentery – broke out which thinned his ranks considerably. To cap it all, the English fleet, lacking favourable winds, was unable to penetrate the Forth. The grand army turned wearily about and returned to England. En route, several religious houses were laid waste, including those at Holyrood, Melrose and Dryburgh.

Near Byland Abbey, 5 miles to the east of Thirsk, Edward paused. He had lost 16,000 men and was desperately in need of fresh troops. To this end, he issued instructions that all fighting men between the ages of sixteen and sixty should flock to his banner. Unknown to him, however, Robert the Bruce was hot on his trail. Having crossed the border, the Scots captured Norham Castle and pillaged several towns, including Northallerton, on their march south.

On 14 October, the Scots discovered the English army – camped to the north of Byland Abbey, on Oldstead Moor. The resulting battle was a scrappy, disorganised affair. The high ground occupied by the English should have rendered their position virtually impregnable and the Scots scrambling up the hillside were, indeed, beaten back by heavy assaults from the English archers. Unfortunately, the English leaders, the Earls of Pembroke and Richmond, were so preoccu-

Byland Abbey was pillaged by the Scots after the Battle of Byland in 1322, but survived until 1539 when, at the Dissolution of the Monasteries, it was stripped of all its assets and consigned to centuries of neglect and decay.

pied with repelling the frontal assault that they paid no heed to their rear. A number of Scots, forming a flanking party, scaled the hill at another point under cover of woodland and were able to sweep down on the defenders from behind. The resulting confusion within the English ranks enabled the main body of Scots to reach the top of the hill. Thus surrounded, panic took root in the English ranks and the army was put to flight. It is reported that a terrible slaughter took place, with the survivors being pursued as far as the gates of York.

While the battle was raging, Edward, seemingly unaware of the situation, was dining at the Abbey itself. When news of the defeat reached him, he left the remnants of his army, fleeing first to York and then to Bridlington. The Scots ransacked Byland and discovered, to their delight, that Edward had also abandoned the crown jewels. After looting Byland and nearby Rievaulx Abbey, the invaders moved south, burning and pillaging as far south as Beverley, before retreating into Scotland, unmolested, a week later.

The blame for the English defeat was laid at the door of Andrew de Harcla, the hero of the Battle of Boroughbridge. En route to Byland with English reinforcements, his progress had been regrettably slow. Suspected of collusion with the Scots, he was tried and executed. In the longer term, Edward was compelled to conclude a truce with Scotland. Although it did not succeed in putting a stop to endemic border warfare, there was to be no major incursion by the Scots for thirteen years.

The Walk

1. Begin at Byland Abbey. The Abbey, cared for by English Heritage, must have constituted a magnificent spectacle in its day, its wealth and splendour rendering it fit for the entertainment of a king. The marauding Scots were laden with rich treasures, not least with the Abbey's collection of priceless books and manuscripts, which were doubtless cast aside as so much worthless lumber.

2. From the Abbey ruins, walk up the minor road to Oldstead. When you reach Oldstead, bear to the right and walk through the village before striking off to your right along Sand Lane.

Walk 7: Battle of Byland Abbey   35

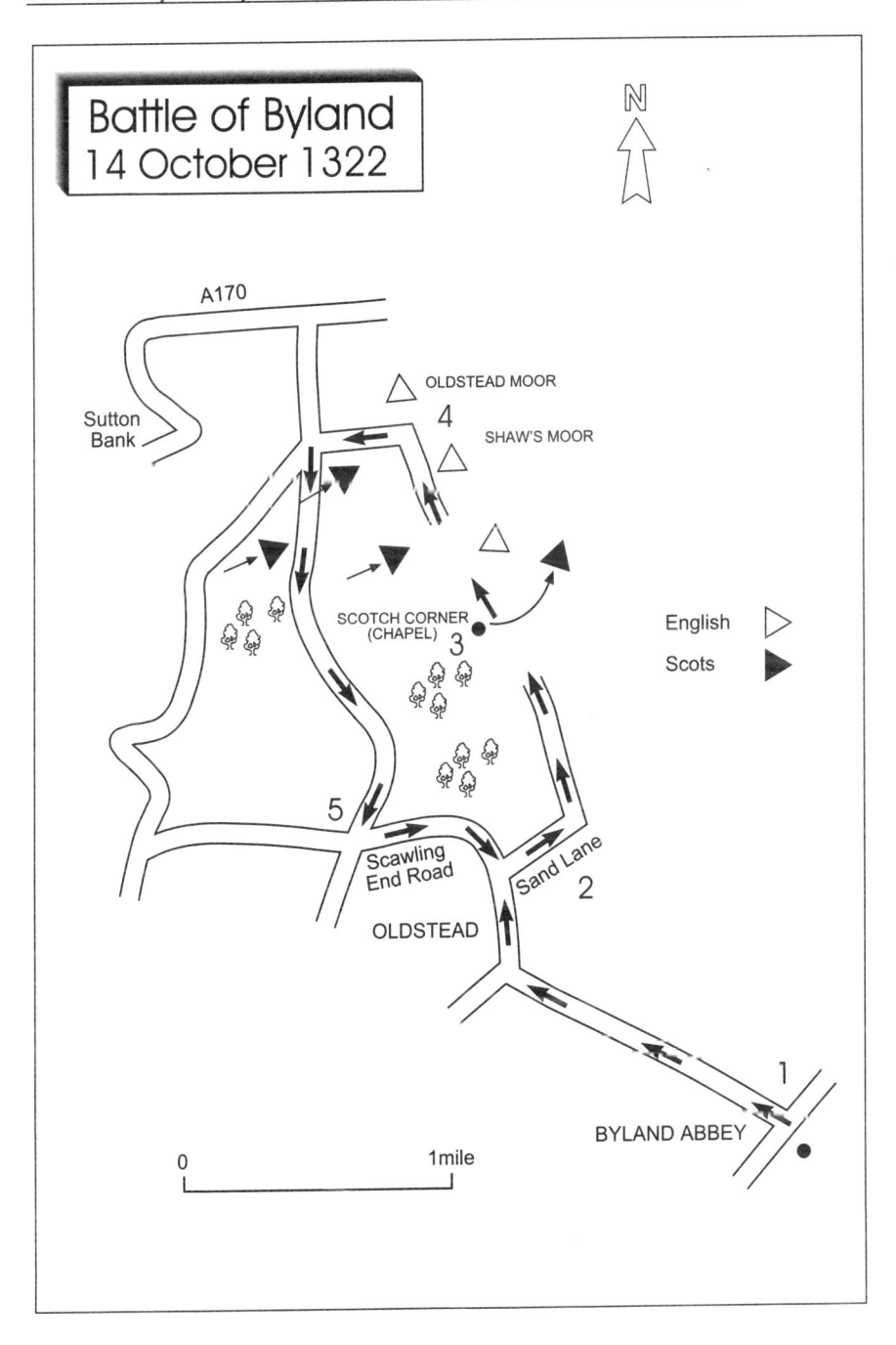

3. Follow Sand Lane which becomes a track climbing steadily up towards Shaw's Moor. En route, on your left, is a small chapel, built as a memorial to students of Ampleforth College who were killed during the Second World War. This point is known locally as 'Scotch Corner' and is generally believed to be the point at which the Scots outflanked the English army.

4. Continue walking along the track which follows Oldstead Bank, a ridge thought to be the scene of heavy fighting. Emerge from the trees onto Shaw's Moor, above which lies Oldstead Moor, upon which the English army was encamped.

5. Follow the track sharply to the left and then turn left again to take the rough track which goes back downhill through the woods. (Halfway down to your left is Silver Fox Farm.) At the bottom, turn to your left to follow the road back into Oldstead and retrace your steps to your starting point at Byland Abbey. As far as battlefields are concerned, Byland may not be the most clinically precise in terms of the information available, but it certainly makes for one of the most attractive walks.

Walk 8: Battle of Bramham

19 February 1408

Route: Bramham – Headley – Camp Hill – Oglethorpe Whin Covert – Bramham

Starting Point: Almshouse Hill, Bramham

Length: 5 miles. Moderate.

Map: Ordnance Survey Explorer 289

Access: Bramham lies on the A1, 4 miles south of Wetherby. Parking available in the village.

About the Walk

The Wars of the Roses, chronicling the rivalry between the House of Lancaster and the House of York, are usually said to have begun in 1455 with the Battle of St Albans. In fact, hostilities may be said to have started much earlier, and it is arguable that the civil wars opened in 1408, with the Battle of Bramham Moor.

The succession to the English throne was clear cut down to Edward III, who had four sons with legitimate claims. His eldest son, Edward, the 'Black Prince', pre-deceased him by one year. The second son was Lionel, Duke of Clarence; the third, John of Gaunt; the fourth Edmund, Duke of York. When Edward III died in 1377, the son of the 'Black Prince' – the 10 year old Richard – became king. He reigned until 1399 when he was deposed and imprisoned in Pontefract Castle by Henry of Bolingbroke, son of John of Gaunt, who seized the throne and was crowned Henry IV. In February 1400, Richard's death was announced, giving rise to rumours that he had been murdered on Henry's orders. Such rumours led, in turn, to open rebellion, spear-headed by a powerful faction of nobles, including Henry Percy, Earl of Northumberland, Thomas Mowbray, Earl Marshall of England, Sir William Plumpton and the lords Bardolph, Hastings and Falconbridge.

Another prominent rebel was Richard Scrope, Archbishop of

York. Through his preaching and ecclesiastical influence, he stirred up a hornets' nest. Carried along on a wave of public enthusiasm, he found himself, in the spring of 1405, encamped on Shipton Moor with 20,000 men. The Earl of Westmoreland, acting for Henry, marched to Shipton with a view to putting an end to the uprising. Although he had a strong force at his disposal, Westmoreland found the rebels occupying a strong defensive position, and resorted to subterfuge in order to overcome them. Pretending to agree to their demands, he persuaded Scrope to dismiss his men. As soon as he had done so, he and Mowbray were arrested. Scrope's followers were also caught off guard and many were killed by Westmoreland's men. Scrope, Mowbray, Falconbridge, Hastings and Plumpton were executed.

Through visiting battlefields, we often become acquainted with localities we might otherwise never have known. In this connection, no rural walk is complete without a visit to a country pub, such as the 'Red Lion' in the picturesque village of Bramham.

Northumberland and Bardolph fled into Scotland, beyond the reach of Henry's rough justice. Early in 1408, they returned, leading a substantial army of Scots. Their intention was to overthrow Henry, an objective which conflicted with the behaviour of their troops, who laid waste much of the country through which they passed. At Thirsk, the expedition paused while Northumberland issued an appeal for support from all who were disaffected with the king. The response was less than enthusiastic, and those who did appear were inexperienced and poorly armed.

When Sir Thomas Rokeby, High Sheriff of Yorkshire, learned of the projected rebellion, he acted quickly and gathered together a strong force to occupy the bridge at Knaresborough, in an effort to stop the rebels' progress. Northumberland decided to avoid Knaresborough and made his way, via Wetherby, to Bramham. Rokeby was soon in pursuit, gathering, en route, much of the support for which Northumberland had hoped. On 19 February 1408, Rokeby encountered the rebels deployed on Bramham Moor.

Few details of the action are available, but it is probable that the rebels occupied high ground on Camp Hill. The Scots disliked defensive positions, preferring the impetus of a downhill charge, during which they could accelerate to a collision speed of 12 miles per hour – success depending, in part, upon the fear they inspired. Against disciplined troops who stood their ground, these onslaughts were less effective. We do know that the battle was of relatively short duration and that the superior training of Rokoby's levies must have turned the tide in his favour.

Fatally wounded, Bardolph was captured, but expired shortly afterwards. According to some sources, Northumberland was taken alive and beheaded in York. Others maintain that while trying to escape, he hid in a hollow by Oglethorp Whin Covert and was there discovered and killed. His head, along with that of Bardolph, was sent to London where it was paraded through the streets and placed on London Bridge, to serve as a deterrent to all would-be traitors.

The Walk

1. Begin in the village of Bramham. From Almshouse Hill, walk into Ficoly Lane and across Aberford Road into Headley Lane.

2. Walk down Headley Lane, which crosses Bramham Moor, to Headley. At the junction, turn right into Spen Common Lane. Camp Hill is to the right. The levelling effect of centuries of ploughing are evident on the site of this early hill fort, which may well have been the spot chosen by the rebels to make their stand. Bullets have occasionally been found here – a reminder, perhaps, that the use of gunpowder in early 14th-century battles, although rare, was not unknown. Fighting must have occurred over much of the Moor, and spectral horsemen – attributed to fleeing rebels – have been sighted from time to time.

40   *Battlefield Walks in Yorkshire*

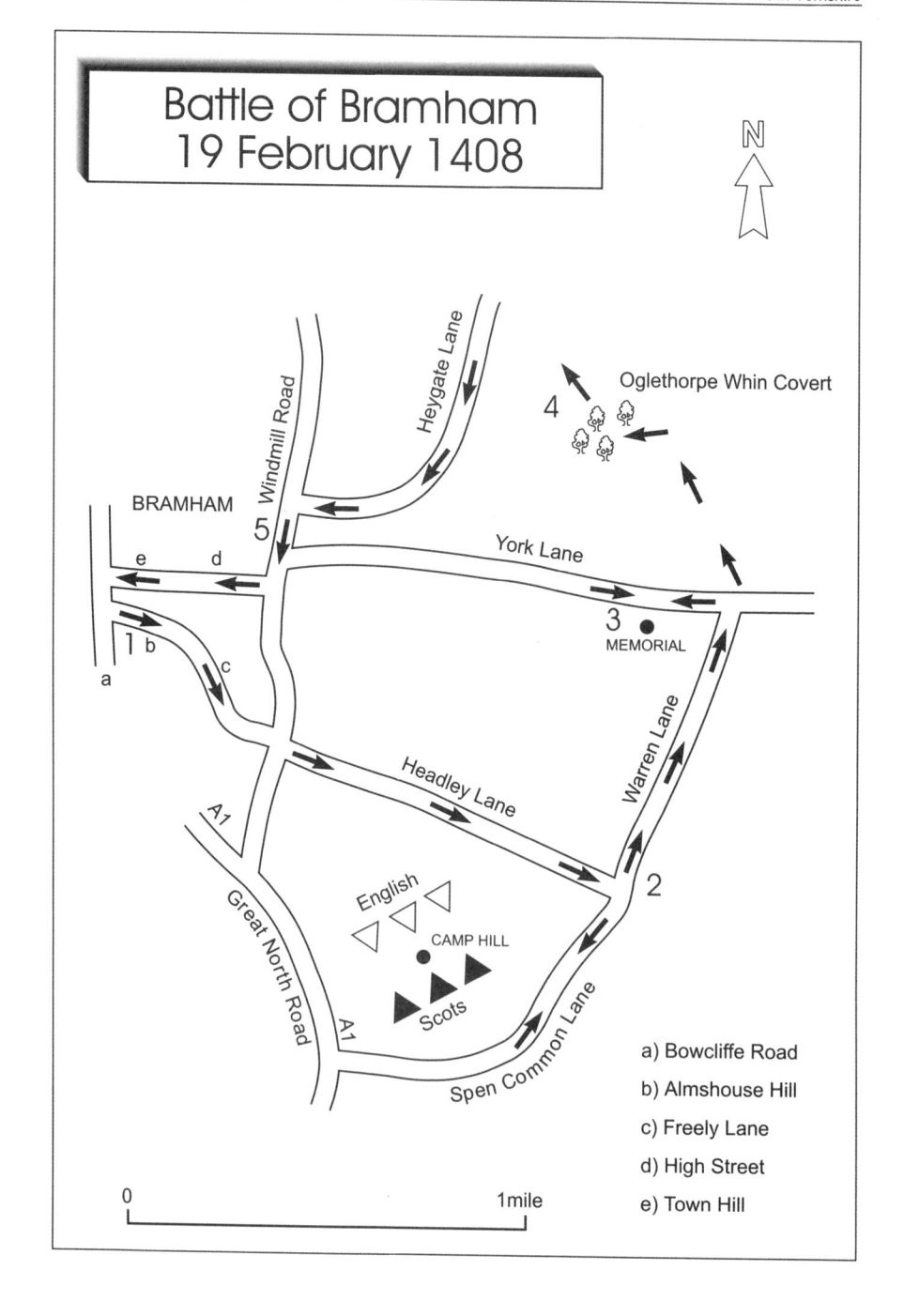

Battle of Bramham
19 February 1408

Oglethorpe Whin Covert

BRAMHAM

Windmill Road

Heygate Lane

York Lane

MEMORIAL

Warren Lane

Headley Lane

English

CAMP HILL

Scots

Great North Road

A1

Spen Common Lane

a) Bowcliffe Road
b) Almshouse Hill
c) Freely Lane
d) High Street
e) Town Hill

0   1mile

3. Retrace your steps up Spen Common Lane into Warren Lane. At the junction, turn left into York Lane. On the left-hand side of the road, hidden in a copse, as Oglethorpe Whin Covert looms up on your right, are the remains of a cross, said to mark the site of Northumberland's death. The spot appears to be used for fly-tipping. Lying amid a heap of household rubbish and covered in graffiti, this is undoubtedly the worst maintained battlefield monument in the British Isles.

4. Retrace your steps to Warren Lane. Take the path opposite Warren Lane, leading to Oglethorpe Hall Farm. The path starts by following two field boundaries. At the end of the second field, strike off along a public footpath to your left in the direction of Oglethorpe Whin Covert. This path runs through the covert and, shortly after clearing the trees, bears to the left. Follow the path to Heygate Lane.

5. Turn left down Heygate Lane and continue walking into Windmill Road which eventually runs into Aberford Road. Turn right into High Street and walk up to Town Hill, which dovetails with Almshouse Hill and your starting point.

Walk 9: Battle of Wakefield

30 December 1460

Sandal – Wakefield – Sandal

Starting Point: Sandal Castle. Car parking in the Castle grounds.

Length: 3 miles. Strenuous.

Map: Street Plan of Wakefield.

Access: Sandal Castle lies 2 miles to the south of Wakefield on the A61 Barnsley road. Look out for the 'Sandal Castle' sign at the junction with Manygates Lane.

About the Walk

The first major battle of the Wars of the Roses was fought at St Albans in 1455. On that occasion, the White Rose of York overcame the Red Rose of Lancaster.

On 10 October 1460, Richard, Duke of York was recognised as heir to Henry VI, the Lancastrian king. Henry, being of unsound mind, placidly accepted the arrangement, and it was left to his strong-willed queen, Margaret, to try to rectify the situation. Accordingly, she gathered an army of some 15,000 men, which assembled at Pontefract. Richard acted quickly and, in company with one of his sons, Edmund Earl of Rutland, and the Earl of Salisbury, he marched north to his own castle at Sandal, outside Wakefield. En route, near Worksop, his army was ambushed and mauled by a Lancastrian force. Footsore and weary, the Yorkists eventually reached Sandal on 21 December. It is possible that an armistice was arranged so that both sides could celebrate Christmas.

In fact, there was little for the Yorkists to celebrate. As a rule, the fighting season ran from Easter through to mid-September. Outside these months, it was difficult for an army on the move to live off the land. In this instance, whatever produce was available was being snapped up by the Lancastrians, leaving precious few pickings for Richard's 5,000 Yorkists. By 28 December, as the Lancastrians approached Sandal, provisions must have been running dangerously low.

It is often argued that it was in Richard's interests to maintain a defensive position within the castle walls, and it seems that he was advised to do so. Apart from the shortage of food, there was insufficient room for most of his army, which remained camped outside the castle and therefore vulnerable to attack. On the other hand, Richard expected another son, Edward, Earl of March, the future Edward IV, currently in Shrewsbury, to come to his aid. If Sandal could hold out until Edward's arrival, then the Lancastrians would be caught between two forces. Similarly, there was reason to hope that help would come from Lord Neville, who had been raising an army on Richard's behalf. Afraid of becoming trapped and ill-equipped for a protracted siege, the Lancastrians planned to entice Richard into battle. Accordingly, they busied themselves in taunting him from a safe distance.

They also concealed many of their number in surrounding woodland and may even have contrived to introduce a detachment of their own men into the castle. Whatever the truth of the matter, Richard was duped into believing that the Lancastrian army was not up to strength.

The spark which ignited the battle occurred on 30 December, when a Yorkist foraging party was chased back to the castle empty handed. Accordingly, in the early afternoon of that day, he marched out of the castle towards Wakefield Green, to meet what he mistakenly thought was an inferior force. A hail of arrows met the Yorkists as they charged the Lancastrian lines in what was clearly an attempt to push the enemy into the River Calder. Richard appeared to be succeeding yet, as soon as he was committed, more Lancastrians emerged from the woods on both Yorkist flanks, cutting off his retreat to the castle.

Surrounded and outnumbered, the Yorkists bravely fought on. Then, with the situation deteriorating, Lord Neville's newly recruited force of 8,000 men appeared on the scene. To Richard's horror, they joined the Lancastrian ranks. In the face of such overwhelming odds, many Yorkists began to quit the field. Richard himself chose to die fighting, his back to a willow tree. The battle lasted for only an hour or so, but the pursuit and slaughter of the fleeing Yorkist rank and file continued into the early evening.

His head was severed on the orders of Lord Clifford, sometime Yorkist and now a leading Lancastrian. Bearing a crown fashioned out of paper, the head was placed on the ramparts of Micklegate Bar in York. Clifford is also credited with killing the young Earl of Rutland, hacked to death on Wakefield Bridge while trying to escape. In total, over 2,000 Yorkists lost their lives.

The Walk

1. Begin at Sandal Castle which, like many another magnificent stronghold, was destroyed by the Roundheads after the Civil War. Apart from the earthworks, precious few crumbling fragments of masonry survive to remind us of its greatness. To get your bearings, take a preliminary amble around the perimeter path. Look out to the north-west. Beneath you, the Yorkists marched out to meet the visible Lancastrian force to the north of the present-day Country Park. To the Yorkists' right, in the locality of the new housing development – at that time, woodland – was a second Lancastrian force. To their left, hidden in more woodland, was a third Lancastrian contingent – an area now partially covered by the Country Park's water feature.

2. After visiting the new (Summer 2002) Visitor Centre, turn left into Manygates Lane. Continue across Castle Road and pause at the Youth Centre – formerly a school – opposite the recreation ground. Adjacent to the pavement, within the Youth Centre grounds, is a memorial to the Duke of York who 'fighting for the cause of the white rose fell on this spot in the battle of Wakefield December 30th 1460.' The present monument, erected in 1897, replaced an earlier one demolished during the Civil War. The site itself is still reputed to be haunted.

3. Continue walking to the junction with the A61. Turn left and walk towards Wakefield. The approach to the River Calder, along Bridge Street, acquired the name 'Fall Ings', owing to the heavy fatalities among the fleeing Yorkists which occurred here. Beyond Bridge Street is the bridge over the River Calder. To the right is St Mary's Chapel. Founded in 1356-57, it is supposed to

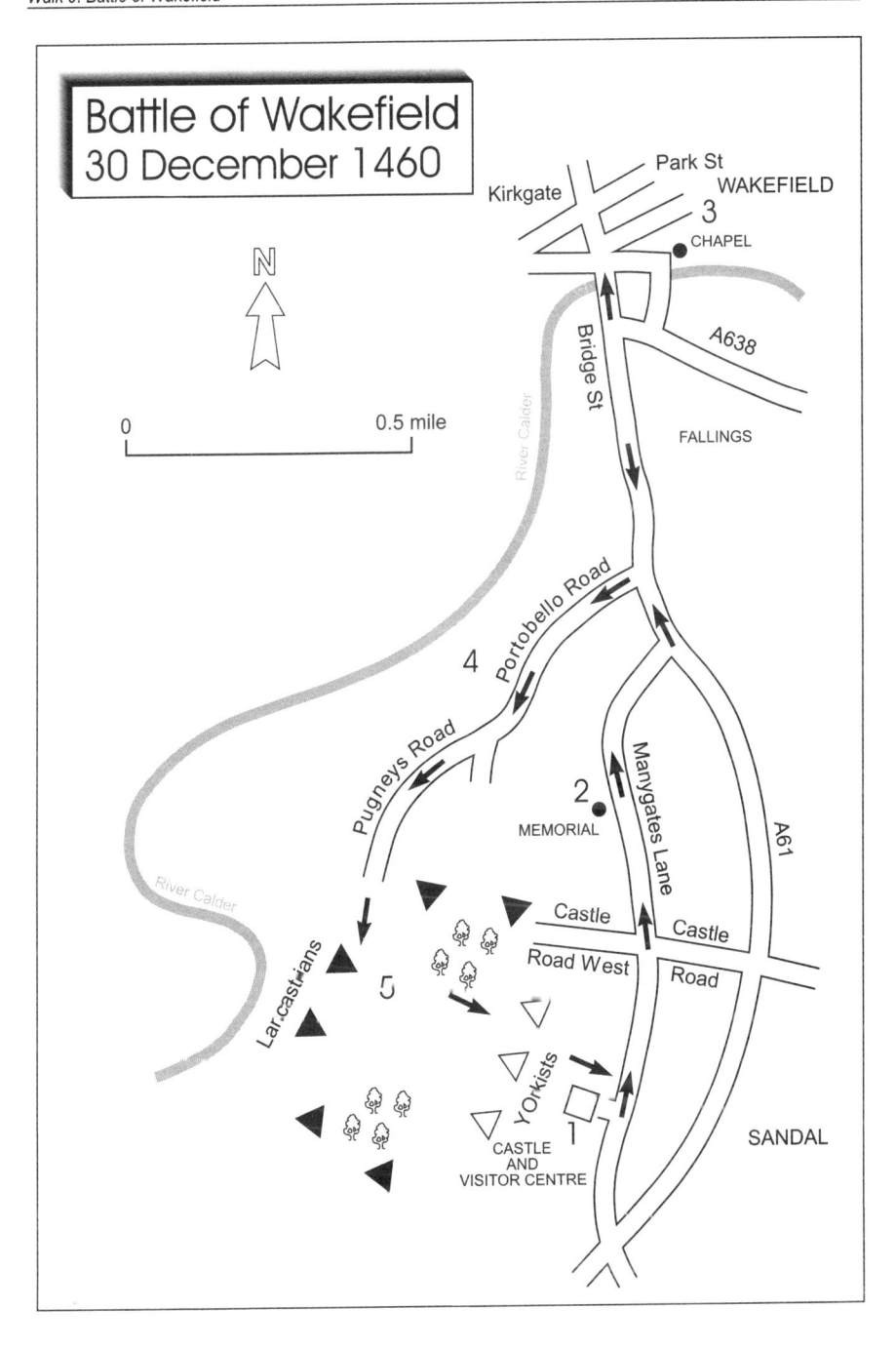

Walk 9: Battle of Wakefield 45

Battle of Wakefield
30 December 1460

have been enriched by Edward IV, in memory of his father and brother. Rutland was killed by Clifford very near to the bridge – according to some sources slightly further north, near the junction of Kirkgate and Park Street.

4. Retrace your steps down Bridge Street and the A61. Turn to the right to walk up Portobello Road, running parallel with the River Calder. A good many relics of the battle – bones, swords etc – were unearthed along here in 1825 during the construction of Portobello House, now demolished. One would have imagined that the Yorkists were boxed in, but the evidence suggests that the fighting was dispersed over a fairly wide area. Keep walking into Pugneys Road and on to the footpath.

The monument, erected in 1867, to commemorate the death of Richard Duke of York, marks the site of Richard's last stand. The column replaced a wooden cross, erected in 1461 and destroyed in 1645 during the English Civil War.

5. Walk straight on to the footpath at the conclusion of Pugneys Road. Just beyond the building line, turn left along a straight path which crosses Milnthorpe Lane and leads up to Sandal Castle. This is a fairly strenuous climb, but by approaching the castle from this direction, you can acquire a good impression of its eminence and also of the Yorkist/Lancastrian positions. An easier return can be made by turning left into Milnthorpe Lane and walking round into Castle Road West and Manygates Lane.

Walk 10: Battle of Ferrybridge
28 March 1461
Ferrybridge – Brotherton – Ferrybridge

Starting Point: Car Park in Hinton Lane, off Stranglands Lane.

Length: 2½ miles. Easy.

Maps: Ordnance Survey Explorer 289 & 290.

Access: Ferrybridge lies to the north of the Ferrybridge Service Area at the junction of the A1 and the M62.

About the Walk

One of the most remarkable facts about the Wars of the Roses is that no sooner had one side suffered a seemingly crushing defeat than it bounced back into contention. At Wakefield, on 30 December 1460, the White Rose of York had been trampled underfoot. Its head, Richard, Duke of York, had been slain and the victorious Lancastrian army ran riot, sacking and pillaging its way to London. Unfortunately for the Lancastrians, two prominent Yorkists were still at large. One was the late Richard's son and heir, Edward, Earl of March who now became Duke of York. The other was the redoubtable Earl of Warwick whose efforts to place Edward on the throne of England would earn him the title of 'kingmaker.'

Despite their triumph at Wakefield, the Lancastrians were unable to gain entry to London. Stories of their depredations preceded them and the citizens thought it expedient to pledge their allegiance to the Yorkists. The Lancastrians, led by their queen, Margaret of Anjou and her feeble minded husband, Henry IV, had no choice but to retreat once more into Yorkshire. Edward and Warwick were soon in hot pursuit. By the time they reached Pontefract Castle on 26 March 1461, the Yorkist army was 40,000 strong. From their headquarters at York, the Lancastrians marched out to meet them and, with an army of 60,000 men, took up position to the south of Tadcaster, at Towton.

From their base at Pontefract Castle, the Yorkists despatched a force commanded by Lord Fitzwalter to secure a passage over the River Aire, two and a half miles away, at Ferrybridge. Arriving on the afternoon of 27 March 1461, Fitzwalter dispersed a party of Lancastrians who were arrayed on the north bank overlooking the bridge spanning the river and set up camp.

Early on the following morning, Fitzwalter was roused from his bed by the sound of fighting. Thinking that it was a fracas among his own men, he emerged bleary-eyed, to be cut down almost immediately by a contingent of Lancastrians, led by Lord Clifford. At the head of 500 of his light cavalry – 'The Flower of Craven' as they were known – Clifford had mounted a surprise assault on Fitzwalter's poorly defended position.

While Clifford broke the bridge and prepared to defend the north bank of the Aire, the surviving Yorkists retreated to Pontefract. Rallying their army, Edward and Warwick decided to advance on Ferrybridge and Clifford's position. When they arrived, at some point in the afternoon of 28 March, they came under attack from the Lancastrian archers. The Yorkist archers returned fire while their engineers pondered methods of plugging the gap Clifford had made in the bridge.

Eventually, a makeshift walkway was constructed and a massed group of Yorkists edged forward in an attempt to put it in place. Such was the firepower of the Lancastrian archers, however, that all efforts failed, resulting in heavy Yorkist casualties. Among the latter was the Earl of Warwick who sustained an arrow wound in the leg as he personally led a desperate charge towards the bridge.

In view of the impossibility of taking the bridge by a frontal assault, an alternative plan was devised. This involved sending Lord Fauconberg with 1,000 men to cross the river three miles higher up, at Castleford and to take Clifford in the rear. Fauconberg effected the crossing, but Clifford's scouts got wind of his approach and the Lancastrians, fearful of being caught between the two Yorkist forces, began a retreat towards their main army at Towton.

Warwick was now able to cross the bridge and, together with Fauconberg, began a pursuit of Clifford and his 'Flower of Craven.' It was Fauconberg who caught up with Clifford, at Dintingdale – tanta-

It was usual for the casualties of a War of the Roses battle to be interred in pits, dug on the battlefield itself. Noblemen – whenever they could be identified – were often buried in local churchyards. In 1781, a chalice, a spur and some armour, supposedly belonging to Lord Fitzwalter, were uncovered in St Edward's churchyard at Brotherton.

lisingly close to the safety of the Lancastrian camp. Clifford's men were all but wiped out. He himself was hit in the throat by a bodkin arrow, the 15th-century equivalent of the 'dum dum' bullet, which would divide and spread out on impact. With his death, the Battle of Ferrybridge was brought to a close and the death at Clifford's hands of the young Earl of Rutland at the Battle of Wakefield three months before, avenged.

The Walk

1. Begin at the Car Park in Hinton Lane, by the power station. At the junction with Stranglands Lane, turn left. Just beyond the railway bridge, on the left, is the Old Great North Road and the old bridge in a landscape now dominated by the flyover.

2. There has been a bridge at this location since at least the eleventh century. William the Conqueror crossed the river here on

50 Battlefield Walks in Yorkshire

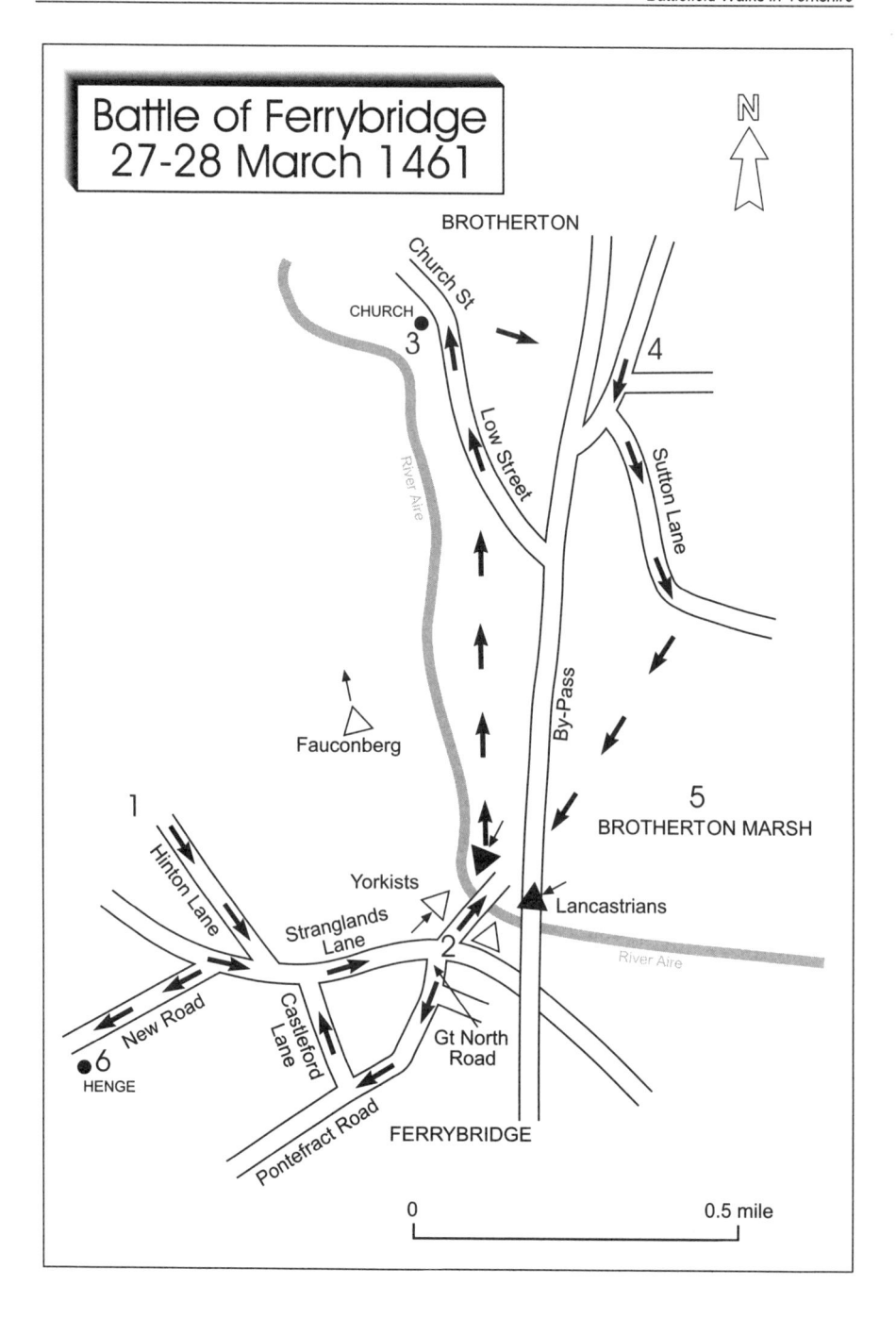

his march north after the Battle of Hastings and, in 1645, a skirmish took place between Royalists and Roundheads contending for control of the bridge. The surviving bridge dates from 1804, but the bridge of the 1461 Battle of Ferrybridge was a wooden structure, built at the end of the 14th century. Walk over the bridge and turn sharp left, to follow the riverside path to Brotherton.

3. At the end of the path, turn left into Low Street and continue to the Church of St Edward. It was in the churchyard, in 1781, that a chalice, a spur and some armour belonging, it was believed, to Lord Fitzwalter were uncovered. As it was the custom for lords who fell in battle to be buried locally, this may well be true.

4. From the church, follow the path from the corner of Church Street which runs over both the railway line and the flyover, to emerge at a roundabout on another surviving portion of the Old Great North Road.

5. Walk down Sutton Lane. Beyond Primrose Dene on your right is another footpath. Walk along here, crossing Marsh Drain. To your left is Brotherton Marsh. Skeletons, armour and other artefacts have also been located in the marsh, probably marking the mass grave of the common soldiers slain in the battle. Continue walking towards the flyover, passing beneath it to join the old bridge once more.

6. Walk back across the bridge and across Stranglands Lane, to continue along the Old Great North Road and the route taken by the Yorkists on their march from Pontefract. Turn into Castleford Lane, to your right, beyond the public library and then left into Stranglands Lane. Walk on, past Hinton Lane, beyond the school and into New Lane. Here is the site of Ferrybridge Henge. After viewing, return to your starting point in Hinton Lane.

Walk 11: Battle of Towton

29 March 1461

Route: Saxton – Lead – Towton – Saxton

Starting Point: Church of All Saints, Saxton

Length: 7 miles. Moderate.

Maps: Ordnance Survey Explorer 289 & 290

Access: Towton is mid-way between York and Leeds, tucked away between the A162 Tadcaster-Ferrybridge road and the B1217. It is easily accessible from the A1, with which it follows a parallel course. On road parking in Saxton.

About the Walk

The Battle of Towton, in which up to 30,000 combatants lost their lives, was the bloodiest encounter of the Wars of the Roses. It followed hard on the heels of the Battle of Ferrybridge, the final phase of which resulted in the death of the Lancastrian, Lord Clifford at Dintingdale, near Saxton. The Yorkist victor of this fight, Lord Fauconberg, may well have lingered in the vicinity of Saxton to await the main Yorkist army of Edward, Duke of York and the Earl of Warwick, which straggled in from Ferrybridge during the evening of 28 March. In contrast to the Lancastrians who were settled in a little to the north, at Towton, the Yorkists must have passed but a poor night.

On the bitterly cold morning of 29 March – Palm Sunday – the Yorkists deployed their troops in two ranks to the north of Saxton village. The front rank consisted of archers, behind whom was the main body, commanded in the centre by Lord Fauconberg. Although outnumbered, the Yorkists were expecting the Duke of Norfolk with their rearguard, from Ferrybridge. Ranged out before them were the Lancastrians – archers also to the fore – commanded by the Duke of Somerset. An additional contingent of Lancastrians lay secluded in Castle Hill Wood, on the Yorkists' left flank. As they prepared for battle, both sides were given instructions that no prisoners were to be taken. And it began to snow.

Towards mid-morning, the Yorkist archers – a strong wind in their favour – advanced and fired a volley of arrows, many of which found their mark. The Lancastrian archers, however, handicapped by firing into the wind, saw their shafts falling well short of the Yorkist lines. Towards 10.00am, realising that his archers could not compete, Somerset ordered his main body forward, pushing forward against the driving snow. The Yorkist front line weathered the initial Lancastrian charge, and savage hand to hand fighting ensued, the Lancastrian front lines hurled onward by the pressure of the surging hordes in the rear. This continued all morning, a gargantuan trial of strength, with the advantage swaying back and forth as the tightly packed mass of 100,000 men battled for survival.

At midday, the Lancastrians launched their ambush from Castle Hill Wood, and, inevitably, the Yorkist left flank was forced to give ground. Although Edward himself played a prominent role in the battle, riding back and forth within his front lines, the Yorkist situation looked perilous, but the status quo was preserved with the arrival at about 4.00pm of the Duke of Norfolk. And so, the combat continued into the afternoon.

At some stage late in the day – probably at around 6.00pm – the Lancastrians began to give ground. Perhaps it started with the desertion of one man whose withdrawal may have been observed by a comrade who himself slipped away – followed by two and then three others until the steady trickle developed into full-blown flight. For many in the rearguard, there had been no opportunity to engage in the fighting, but now they were borne along on a rising tide of retreat, down towards the River Cock. Many hastened through Towton and on to Old London Road, where they hoped to cross the river by Cock Bridge and make their way to York. In this intention, they were severely hampered by sheer weight of numbers, and the pursuing Yorkists, mindful of the command that no quarter should be given, had little difficulty in cutting them down.

All that night and for most of the next day, the pursuit continued. So great was the slaughter that, as one European commentator gleefully observed, it would be many years before England could muster the manpower to engage in any overseas war. As a result of his victory, Edward was crowned King Edward IV, while Margaret and Henry fled north to fight another day. Despite the dreadful carnage of Towton, the Wars of the Roses were far from at an end.

The Walk

1. Begin at the crossroads in the centre of Saxton. Walk along Dam Lane to the B1217 (Towton Lane). Turn left and walk down to the 'Crooked Billet' public house – a name which has its origins in the Yorkist Earl of Warwick's coat of arms. In fact, an earlier inn on this site may have served as the Yorkist headquarters during the battle.

2. From the 'Crooked Billet', cross the road and take the bridleway, Chantry Lane. Negotiate a stile to take you into the field to your right and walk over to St Mary's Chapel, known locally as Lead Church. Although 14th century in origin, the chapel has no known link with the battle. In 1982, however, the Richard III Society reglazed one of the windows, which now bears a representation of Richard's crest – a white boar.

3. Retrace your steps back to the road and turn left, towards Towton. When you reach the junction with Cotchers Lane, you are on the left flank of the Yorkist lines. To your far left is Castle Hill Wood, the position taken by the Lancastrian ambush party.

4. Walk on, to the centre of the battlefield. The first field boundary on the right-hand side of the road beyond Cotchers Lane is adjoined by a rough farm track. At the time of the battle, there stood towards the end of this track, an elderberry tree from which a boy shot an arrow which killed a prominent Lancastrian, Lord Dacre of Gilsland. In the true spirit of legend, the solitary tree which stands at the spot today is said to be a descendant of the original. Opposite this track, on the opposite side of the road is a rectangular field once known as 'The Field of the White Rose and the Red'. Here, many fleeing Lancastrians were slaughtered as they made for the River Cock and it is said

Walk 11: Battle of Towton 55

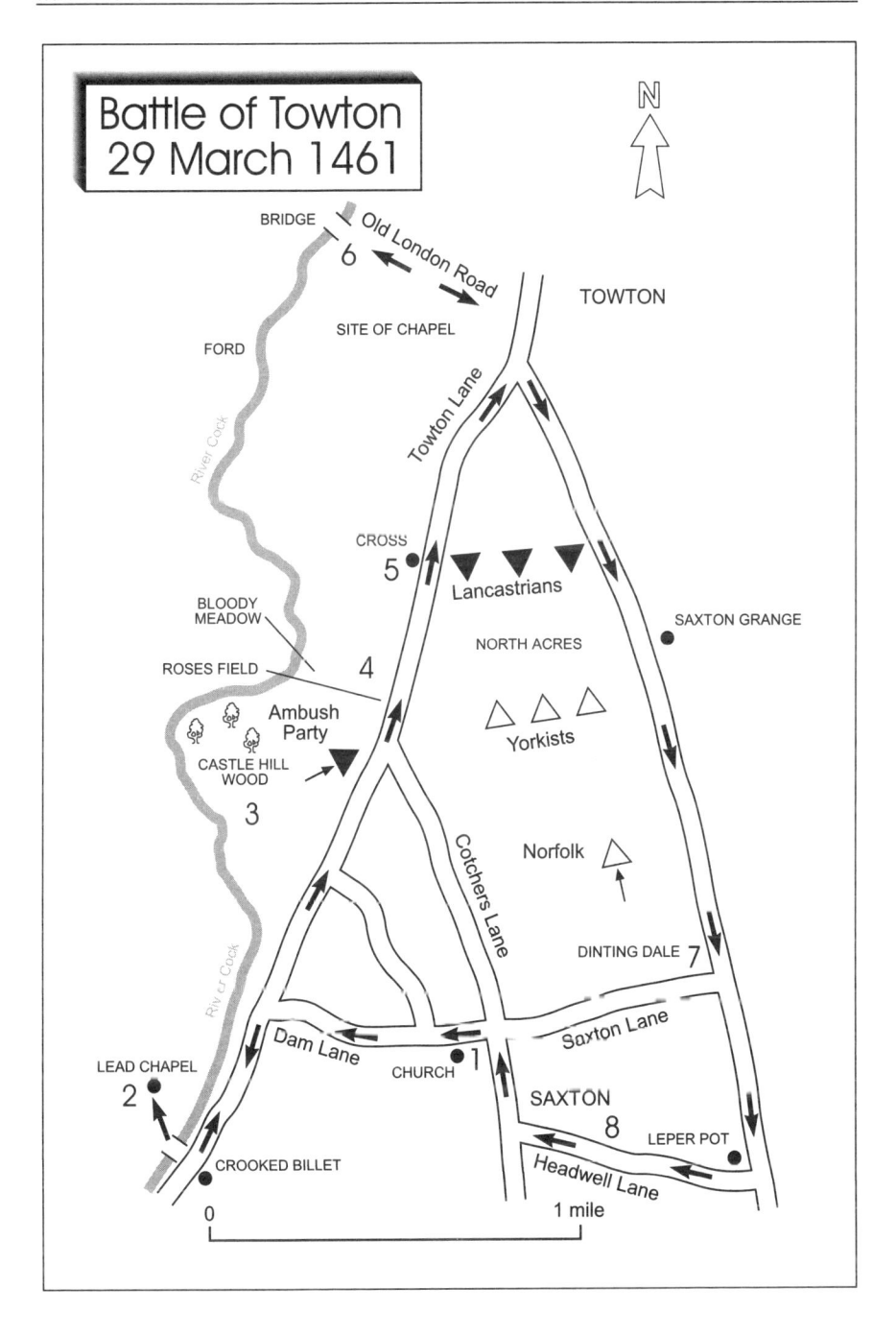

that the delicately formed wild white roses growing there, being imbibed with Lancastrian blood, took on a reddish hue. If you visit the battlefield in the spring or early summer months, you will see these roses growing along the grass verges bordering Towton Lane.

5. Continue to Lord Dacre's Cross, erected in 1928 as a monument to the battle and roughly marking the Lancastrian positions. At the end of the track adjoining the cross is an information board, erected by the Towton Battlefield Society, bearing a map of the battle. Walk on into the village of Towton. On your left is Towton Hall and, to its rear, Chapel Hill, named after a chapel built by Richard III as a memorial to the Towton dead. Before the chapel was completed, Richard was killed at Bosworth, and nothing now remains. Lord Dacre's Cross is thought to be a relic of the chapel. The spot marks one of the battle's burial pits. From time to time, when work is being carried out in the Hall grounds, bodies are disinterred. The latest – 43 in number – were discovered in 1996.

The tomb of Lord Dacre in the churchyard at Saxton. The flowers have been placed there by the Towton Battlefield Society. The small wooden cross (bottom left) commemorates the unknown Yorkist and Lancastrian dead who were buried in pits on the north side of the churchyard.

6. At the 'Rockingham Arms', turn left into the lane known as Old London Road. Continue on to the bridge over the Cock Beck, which occupies the site of an earlier bridge thought to have been used by the fleeing Lancastrian rearguard. Retrace your steps to the main road and through the village. Instead of returning along Towton Lane, take the A162 Ferrybridge road. This is a busy road, but there is a hard path on the left-hand side for part of the way and a grass verge for the remainder. (On your left is Saxton Grange farm, scene of an infamous 1933 murder, when the owner, Freddy Morton, was shot to death. The chauffeur, who was having an affair with Brown's wife, did it.)

7. Continue to Saxton Lane. The Ordnance Survey maps show 'Dinting Dale' transected by Saxton Lane – which should be where Lord Clifford was trapped and killed. Nineteenth-century excavations here supposedly uncovered the remains of both Clifford and the Battle of Wakefield's Yorkist traitor, Lord Neville. However, continue along the A162 to Barkston Ash. On your right, at the corner of the A162 and Headwell Lane, is the base of a cross, curiously known locally as 'The Leper Pot'. It may, at one time, have supported a cross erected to commemorate Clifford's death in the vicinity. The spot is, of course, a little further from the Lancastrian camp and would help in explaining why no one came to Clifford's aid.

8. Walk along Headwell Lane, turning right into Saxton and on to the churchyard of All Saints. Many of the slain are buried here, including Lord Dacre, whose tomb in the churchyard is prominent. It was said that he was buried standing upright and that his horse was buried with him, both of which traditions were apparently proved to be correct when the tomb was disturbed during the 19th century – on which occasion other remains, believed to be those of other casualties, less privileged than Dacre but more privileged than those cast into pits. Some of the bones from the 1996 Towton Hall excavation have also recently been buried here.

Walk 12: Skirmish at Wetherby
30 November 1642
Route: Wetherby Old Town

Starting Point: Wetherby Bridge

Length: 1 mile. Easy.

Map: Wetherby Street Plan

Access: Wetherby lies on the A1, 13 miles to the west of York. Car park and picnic area adjacent to the Bridge.

About the Walk

In November 1642, the first winter of the English Civil War, Lord Fairfax and his son, Sir Thomas, were assembling troops for Parliament in the West Riding. Having amassed a modest force of 1,000 men, Lord Fairfax established his field command at Tadcaster, about 8 miles to the south west of York. Sir Thomas was despatched to Wetherby with 300 Foot and 40 Horse in order to secure the bridge.

Until 1959, Wetherby occupied a key position on the Great North Road. During the early months of the Civil War, the town – commanding the bridge spanning the River Wharfe – was occupied by the Roundheads as part of an effort to isolate Royalist York.

Walk 12: Skirmish at Wetherby

Being appraised of this shrewd move, the Lieutenant-General of the Royalist forces in the North, the Earl of Cumberland, despatched 800 Horse and Foot from York under Sir Thomas Glenham, to secure Wetherby for the King. The force approached stealthily under cover of surrounding woodland at about 6.00am on 30 November 1642. Fairfax was well aware of the problems of defending the town, describing it as a 'place very open ... there being so many back ways to enter in; and friends enough to direct' the enemy.

It was by one of these 'back ways' that a detachment of Royalists gained entry. Most of Fairfax's men were still asleep, quartered in various houses in the town. According to his own account, Fairfax himself was 'on horseback; going out, at the other end of the town, to Tadcaster.....' when the alarm was given. Others claimed he was in the act of putting on his boots. Hurrying to the guardhouse, he found only two infantry sergeants and two pikemen at their arms. At the beginning of the war, he later remarked, 'men were as impatient of Duty as ignorant of it'.

The five of them stood off a charge by Glenham and a handful of men. Despite several shots being fired at Fairfax – and he with only his sword to defend himself – one Royalist officer (Major Carr) was killed and the others driven back. By this time, the Roundhead garrison was coming to its senses and the element of surprise was lost.

In another part of the town, Royalist dragoons under Lieutenant Colonel Norton forced entry. Norton – on foot – was challenged by Royalist Captain Atkinson who was on horseback. Atkinson fired at Norton with his pistol, and missed. Norton grabbed Atkinson's sword belt and pulled him to the ground. Each was joined by his own men and a general mêlée ensued, during which both men were beaten to the ground. Atkinson sustained a broken thigh and subsequently died. It was a sad episode for, before the war, Norton and Atkinson had been neighbours and intimate friends.

The Royalists were not having an easy time of it but, at a critical juncture, Fairfax's powder magazine was hit and blew up. This frightened the Royalists into believing that the Roundheads possessed cannon and they began to retreat. With such Horse as he was able to muster, Fairfax gave chase, pursuing the Royalists for some miles and taking several prisoners.

It had been a minor action. Fairfax lost about ten men, of whom seven had been killed in the explosion. The Roundheads had been caught napping and it was more by good luck than sound management that they had emerged winners, yet Parliament's propaganda machine made the most of a much-needed victory, lauding Fairfax 'that had the gallantist on our side'. As with all his successes, Fairfax himself ascribed it to 'the powerful hand of GOD'.

The Walk

1. Wetherby occupies a key position on the Great North Road. Until 1959, so a plaque on the bridge reminds us, Wetherby Bridge carried all the traffic using the A1. If we accept Fairfax's story that he was on his way to Tadcaster when the Royalists attacked, then he would have been crossing – or have been about to cross – the bridge. His claim that he 'galloped to the Court of Guard', implies that the HQ was at some distance from the bridge.

2. Walk up North Street to the junction with York Road. The Royalists, arriving from York – probably via Long Marston – would have advanced on the town via present-day North Street.

3. Retrace your steps down North Street. To the east, Wetherby tended to blend gradually into the countryside and the 'back yard' by which some of the Royalists effected an entry would have been situated on your left as you walk back towards the bridge.

4. Turn right into St James's Street and continue into Crossley Street. Seventeenth-century Wetherby covered a small area and although much of what we see today is Victorian in origin, the narrow streets reflect the cramped nature of the 17th-century settlement. At some point within the complex of thoroughfares, the two friends, Norton and Atkinson, met as enemies.

5. Turn left into Caxton Street, left again into Westgate and continue down into Market Place. Whenever a battle took place in a town, we can say with some certainty that fighting occurred

Walk 12: Skirmish at Wetherby

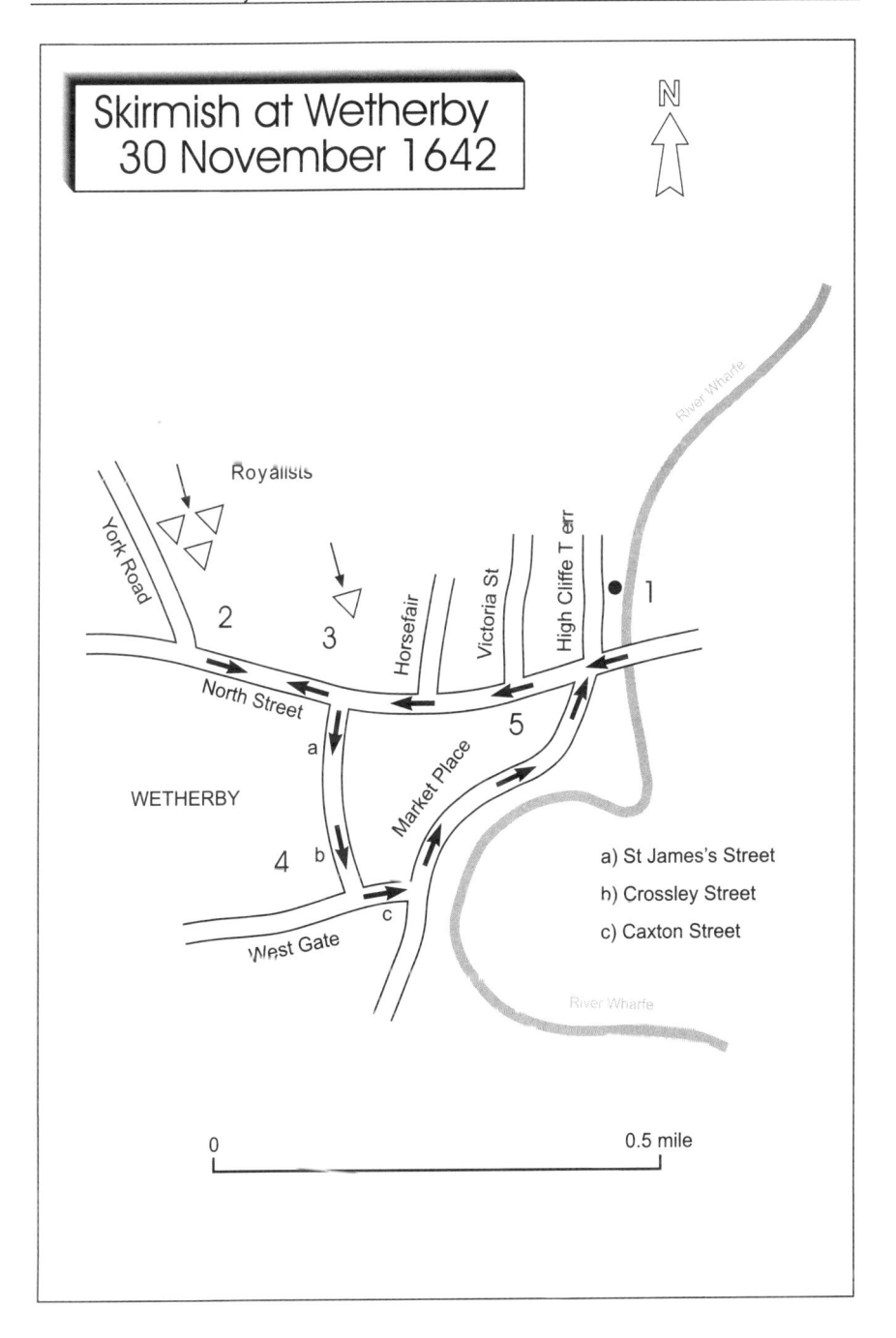

Skirmish at Wetherby
30 November 1642

a) St James's Street
b) Crossley Street
c) Caxton Street

in the market place, by virtue of the available space, otherwise lacking in the narrow streets and alleys. From Market Place, walk back to your starting point at the bridge. The Civil War comprised countless seemingly insignificant skirmishes, of which the action at Wetherby on 30 November 1642, is just one example. In this case, moreover, Fairfax's successful defence did mean that the Roundhead HQ at Tadcaster – see Walk 14 – would not be attacked on two fronts.

Walk 13: Battle of Tadcaster

7 December 1642

Route: Tadcaster town

Starting Point: Car park by Tadcaster Bridge

Length: 2 miles. Moderate.

Map: Ordnance Survey Explorer 290

Access: Tadcaster lies on the A64, 14 miles to the east of Leeds and 10 miles to the west of York. Car parking by Tadcaster Bridge.

About the Walk

In the first week of December 1642 the Earl of Newcastle's Royalist forces, marching from their training ground in the far north, reached York almost unchallenged. Not a man to waste time, Newcastle, who had superseded the Earl of Cumberland as Lieutenant-General of Royalist forces in the North, immediately made plans to attack the Roundhead army of Lord Fairfax. The latter had been contemplating mounting an assault of his own on Royalist York, but Newcastle's approach left him bottled up in his Tadcaster HQ, awaiting the attack which he knew would come.

Fairfax decided that the town itself could not be defended. Tadcaster lay on the west bank of the River Wharf, which was not fordable at that point, rendering a narrow stone bridge the sole means of access from the east bank. Yet, there were no town walls and Fairfax, accompanied by his son, who appears to have retreated from Wetherby, had only 900 men at his disposal. Therefore, he resolved to march out to challenge the Royalists on open ground. Part of the bridge was broken up and artillery placed upon it. Unfortunately, at dawn on 7 December 1642, the Royalists were spotted advancing swiftly from York, down the Roman road known as 'The Old Street'. According to Sir Thomas Fairfax, this meant 'we were necessitated to leave some Foot in a slight Work above the bridge to secure our retreat.' In fact, sheer pressure of Royalist numbers compelled the entire Roundhead force to take refuge behind this last line of defence.

The Royalists saw the Roundhead defences rather differently, Newcastle's wife describing them as constituting 'a very large and strong fort upon the top of a hill, leading eastward ... towards York'. At any rate, they proved enough of a deterrent to discourage Newcastle from risking all upon a frontal assault. He had already decided to send the Earl of Newport and most of his cavalry and dragoons to Wetherby, where they would cross the Wharf to approach Tadcaster in the rear. It was only a matter of time before they would appear on the Roundhead flank. Secure in this knowledge, Newcastle ordered his infantry to attack at 11.00am.

St Mary's Church in Tadcaster. An earlier structure was destroyed by the Scots in 1318, during one of their many incursions south of the border – a reminder of how far south the invaders were able to penetrate, unchallenged.

Fairfax's musketeers served him well and beat back a determined charge, forcing the Royalists to seek the shelter of nearby hedges. Further assaults followed. In one of them, the Royalists managed to gain a foothold in a house by the bridge. This posed a serious problem, for Sir Thomas notes that the Roundheads risked being cut off from their reserves in the town – suggesting that his father's forward position was some distance from the bridge on the east bank. However, a sally mounted by Major-General Gifford drove them off. A second resolute assault 'at another place' was repulsed by a

Captain Lister, who was killed in the process – Sir Thomas describing his death as 'a great loss, being a discreet Gentleman'.

The battle raged throughout the day with such ferocity that the Royalists ran out of powder and match, while the Roundheads asserted that 40,000 musket balls had been exchanged – but Fairfax held on. By 4.00pm, Newcastle was a worried man. Newport had still not arrived and the light was fading. If Newcastle had retained command of the cavalry and dragoons that he had sent with the Earl, he might have succeeded in overrunning the Roundhead positions. As it was, they had been wasted. According to some accounts, Newport, encumbered with artillery, had moved too slowly. Others accused him of treachery. It was also claimed that he was duped into halting by the Roundheads, who sent him a runner with a note bearing Newcastle's forged signature, cancelling the operation. Whatever the reason for his non-appearance, Newcastle had to withdraw for the night.

Under cover of darkness, Fairfax marched to Selby so that when the Royalists advanced to renew their assault the next day, they were able to enter Tadcaster unchallenged. The Roundheads interpreted his action as a sound tactical retreat, Sir Thomas arguing that they 'by the mercy of GOD, were a few delivered from an army who, in their thoughts, had swallowed us up.' In this, there was some truth because although the Royalists had been left in possession of the field of battle, they had failed to destroy Fairfax's force.

The Walk

1. Begin at the car park by the bridge. Turn to your left and cross the bridge.

2. Turn right into Kirkgate. On the left is The Ark, currently a museum/tourist information centre. In the 17th century, it was probably commandeered by the Roundheads.

3. At the top of Kirkgate, turn to the right into the narrow Vicarage Lane, leading to St Mary's Church. The present day church is essentially 19th century, the original building having been destroyed by the Scots during their invasion of 1319 (see Walk 5.

Battle of Tadcaster
7 December 1642

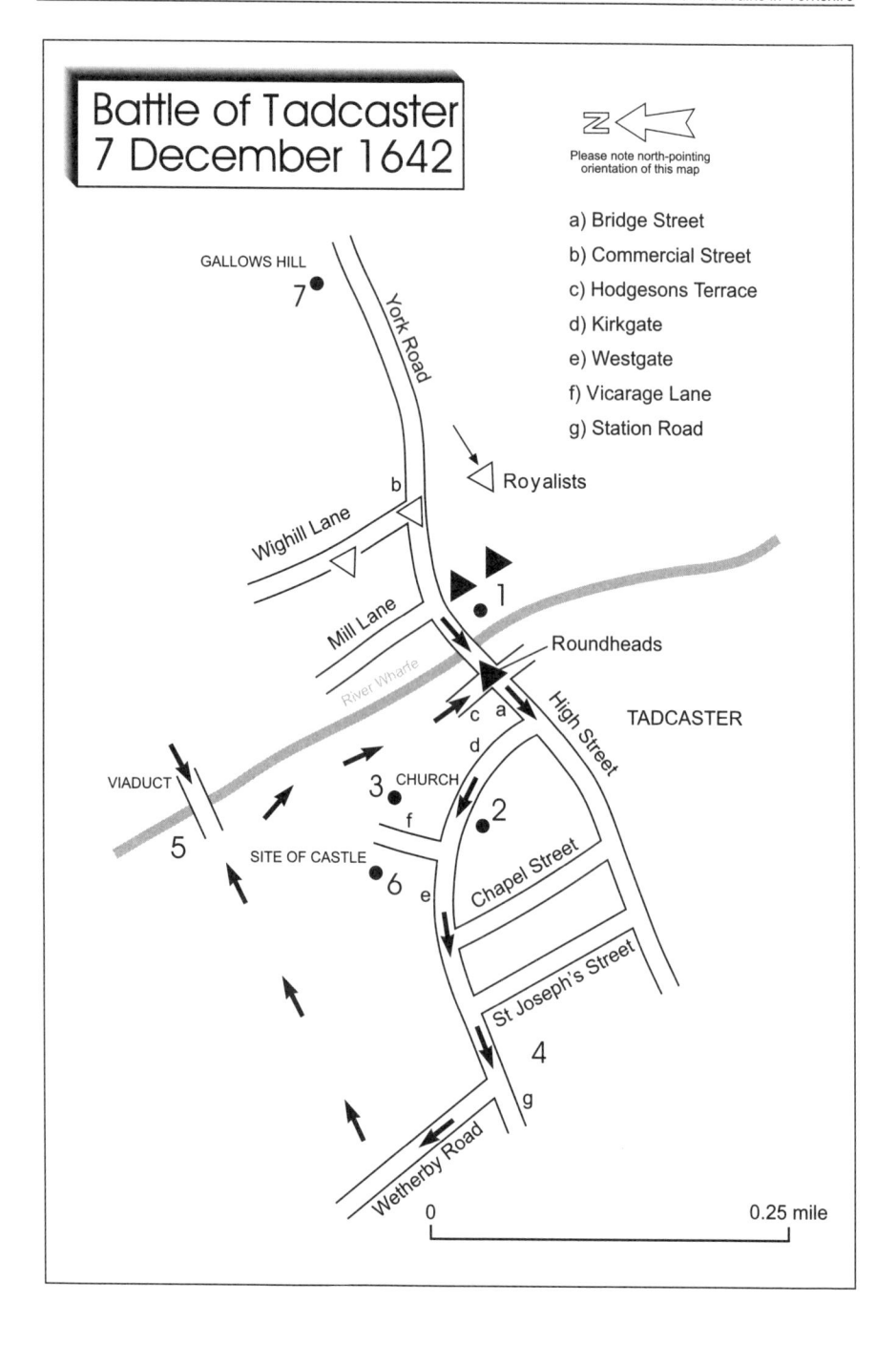

Please note north-pointing orientation of this map

a) Bridge Street
b) Commercial Street
c) Hodgesons Terrace
d) Kirkgate
e) Westgate
f) Vicarage Lane
g) Station Road

GALLOWS HILL 7

York Road

Wighill Lane

Mill Lane

River Wharfe

Royalists

Roundheads

TADCASTER

High Street

VIADUCT

CHURCH

SITE OF CASTLE

Chapel Street

St. Joseph's Street

Wetherby Road

0   0.25 mile

The Battle of Myton). Some of the stones were used in the construction of the bridge.

4. Return to Kirkgate, walk into Westgate and on into Station Road. Defensive entrenchments seem to have run along the line of St Joseph's Street on your left, stretching to the present-day breweries to the south and on to Castle Hill to the north – suggesting that a Royalist attack was expected from the direction of Wetherby and explaining why Sir Thomas had been despatched to Wetherby with instructions to hold it.

5. Turn right into Wetherby Road. Opposite another brewery site is the beginning of the railway viaduct. Built by the railway entrepreneur, George Hudson, in 1849, the line remained unfinished. During the 1990s, it was developed into the Viaduct Walk. Follow the viaduct to the point at which it crosses the river. From here, you have an excellent view of the surrounding countryside.

6. It is possible to cross the river by the viaduct and walk down into the town to return to your starting point. However, I prefer to descend the viaduct via the steps provided and walk across the open ground to the riverside walk, which is part of the Ebor Way. Returning by this route takes you past Castle Hill, nestling behind the trees to your right. Fairfax used the rising ground for gun emplacements.

7. Follow the path past the church, into Hodgsons Terrace and out on to Bridge Street. Turn to the left to cross the bridge and return to the car park. Ahead of you, Commercial Street rises into York Road. On the left is Gallows Hill, which was most probably the point that Fairfax had initially selected for his defence.

Walk 14: Sherburn-in-Elmet
16 December 1642

Route: Sherburn-in-Elmet

Starting Point: Kirkgate, Sherburn-in-Elmet

Length: 3 miles. Moderate.

Map: Ordnance Survey Explorer 290

Access: Sherburn-in-Elmet lies to the east of the A1, on the A162 Tadcaster road. Parking is available off Low Street.

About the Walk

During the latter part of 1642, the Civil War in the North was not going well for the Parliamentarians and the position of the Yorkshire Roundheads, cooped up in Selby, was precarious. Yet, Sir Thomas Fairfax was determined to take the war to the enemy. At 4.00am on 13 December 1642, therefore, in company with Captain John Hotham, he marched out of Selby with a view to raiding the Royalist base at Church Fenton, 6 miles (9.6km) away. When they reached the village, they discovered that the enemy had already departed and so, the next day, they moved on to the neighbouring settlement of Sherburn-in-Elmet.

Their approach over the flat expanse of Sherburn Common was detected by the Royalists, who sent out twenty or thirty cavalrymen to guard what Fairfax describes as 'a Pass near the town'. Fairfax and Hotham had five troops of cavalry and two of dragoons between them – a total of about 300 men – and Fairfax proposed committing them to an attack on this forward detachment of Royalist horse. At about 1.00pm, Fairfax led the charge, putting the Royalists to flight. His scheme was to get in among them and so gain entry to the village.

The Royalist garrison had thrown up a barricade across the main street and, although Fairfax was hot on the heels of the retreating horsemen, they got through the barricade that was immediately closed behind them. The Roundheads now found themselves trapped in what was a narrow lane. Fairfax's horse was shot in the breast. They could not retreat without occasioning considerable confusion within their own ranks and inviting pursuit. The only option was to press forward. In Fairfax's words, they 'stood to it: and stormed the Work with pistol and sword'.

Fairfax noticed that at one end of the barricade, there remained sufficient room for one horse to pass. He forced an entry and his comrades followed. Fortunately, a Royalist troop of cavalry, which should have challenged them, fled. The barricade was taken and the Roundheads rode into the village, carrying all before them. Fairfax's wounded horse collapsed under him, but he obtained another mount and supervised the rounding up of a good many horses and prisoners, including Major-General Windham and Sir William Riddall.

The alarm having been raised, Lord George Goring was approaching with what Fairfax described as 'a good body of Horse', and the Roundhead raiders began an orderly retreat. Goring followed, but at a respectful distance and Fairfax reached Selby virtually unscathed.

In a copybook commando raid, Fairfax had demonstrated that the Yorkshire Roundheads, despite their numerical weakness, were still a force to be reckoned with. And he had bolstered his own growing reputation as Parliament's answer to the Royalist's Prince Rupert – in which capacity, he would soon become known as 'The Rider of the White Horse'.

The Walk

1. Begin in the centre of Sherburn at Kirkgate. Walk down Kirkgate and into Church Hill. The parish church – always open – is an imposing structure, standing atop a hill adjacent to Sir John's Lane. A casual glance at a map gives little indication of Sherburn's strategic value. It is only by visiting the site and standing in the churchyard that you can appreciate the military significance of the panoramic views of the landscape for miles around. It would have been from this vantage point that the Royalists espied Fairfax's approach. Their barricade may have been situated at some point between Sir John's Lane and the lower village.

70 Battlefield Walks in Yorkshire

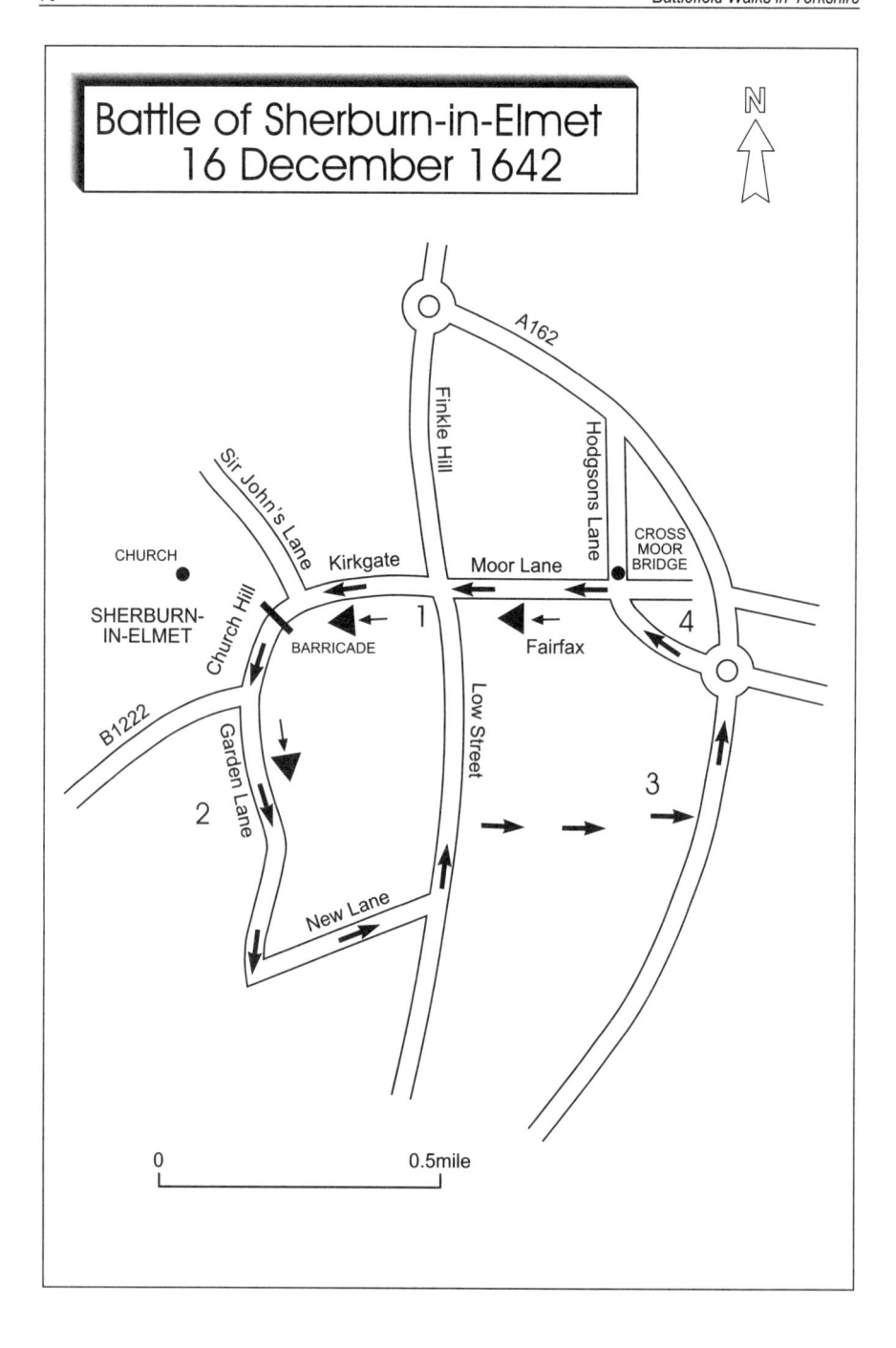

Battle of Sherburn-in-Elmet
16 December 1642

2. Continue walking down Church Hill, following the line of the running battle between the Royalists and the pursuing Roundheads. Walk on into Garden Lane, taking the path to the left of the school. Turn left into New Lane and left again into Low Street.

3. A little way up on the right, opposite High Trees Court, take the track skirting the south of the village. Proceed along the track to the new Sherburn by-pass – the A162. There is no doubt that the by-pass has relieved Sherburn of much heavy traffic, but the potential problem – as with all by-passes – will be the housing developments and industrial estates which could well take root in later years.

Sherburn's parish church dates from the 12th century. Until the middle of the 14th century, it was the seat of the archbishops of York. Commanding panoramic views of the surrounding landscape, the churchyard assumed strategic significance during the Civil War when the village was occupied by Royalist forces.

4. Turn left, along the A162 and walk up to the roundabout. Walk as far as the junction with the old Moor Lane – now a dead-end – which preceded the by-pass. At the junction with Hodgsons Lane is Cross Moor Bridge, the 'Pass' by which Fairfax gained entry to Sherburn. Walk back along Moor Lane, following the preliminary stages of the running fight, which returns you to your starting point at the crossroads.

Walk 15: Adwalton Moor
30 June 1643

Route: Oakwell Hall – Birstall – Adwalton – Drighlington – Oakwell Hall

Starting point: Oakwell Hall Country Park. Car Parking available.

Length: 4 miles. Moderate.

Map: Ordnance Survey Explorer 288

Access: Oakwell Hall is located off the A652 Bradford-Dewsbury road and can be accessed via Junction 27 of the M62.

About the Walk

During the first six months of 1643, the well disciplined Royalist army of the Earl of Newcastle held sway in Yorkshire. Scarborough Castle fell into Royalist hands and it was rumoured that Sir John Hotham, Roundhead Governor of Hull, was considering changing sides. To cap it all, on 30 March, Sir Thomas Fairfax was beaten at the Battle of Seacroft Moor, to the north east of Leeds. In May, there was a temporary reverse of fortune when Fairfax made a successful assault on Wakefield, but in June 1643, Newcastle was again on the offensive.

Newcastle's prime objective was Bradford, the headquarters of Lord Fairfax. On 22 June, he took Howley House, a Roundhead stronghold between Leeds and Wakefield. Then, on the morning of 30 June, with some 9,000 men, he set out for Bradford. Having few provisions, the Fairfaxes, father and son, thought that it would be impossible to defend the town. Accordingly, they decided to march out to meet Newcastle, with the aim of surprising him. They had intended to start out no later than 4.00am on 30 June but did not get under way until much before 8.00am. In fact, they had marched just four miles when they came upon the enemy. Sir Thomas suspected treachery for the Royalists were ready and waiting for them, 'drawn up in Battalia' on a plain by the village of Adwalton.

The Fairfaxes, leading an ill-assorted crew of horse and foot, were outnumbered by three to one. Scattering advance parties of Royalists, they drew up in three divisions – Major General John Gifford on the left, Sir Thomas on the right and Lord Fairfax, in overall command, in the centre. Newcastle's three divisions were deployed over open ground. His left wing was hampered somewhat by open-cast coal mines, while the Roundheads' mobility was compromised by a number of enclosures.

Lord Fairfax did possess one advantage in that he had twice as many musketeers as Newcastle – all experienced men – who he put to good use by deploying them under cover of hedges, which defined the enclosures. There was an opening leading out on to Adwalton Moor, capable of taking about half a dozen horsemen, and a contingent of Royalist cavalry attempted to force its way through. The attempt failed as the horsemen were met by thunderous volleys of musket fire. A second charge was beaten off in similar fashion, the Roundheads giving pursuit.

Sir Thomas's left wing was also gaining ground and Newcastle was on the verge of ordering a retreat when a final desperate charge of Royalist pikemen on Gifford's wing bore fruit. Led by a Colonel Skirton, who Sir Thomas describes as 'a wild and desperate man', the attack sent Gifford's men reeling. Sir Thomas afterwards maintained that the Roundhead left wing was obscured by a ridge, making it difficult to know how Gifford was faring. Therefore, the Roundhead right fought on until they found themselves being outflanked by the Royalists who had broken through Gifford's lines. Lord Fairfax ordered a general retreat and he himself was pursued towards Bradford, while Sir Thomas fled to Halifax.

According to Newcastle, 500 Roundheads were killed at Adwalton Moor and 1400 taken prisoner, while his own casualties – if he is to believed – were remarkably light, with only 22 dead. Despite the unequal contest, the battle was recognised as an important Royalist victory and Newcastle was created Marquis of Newcastle soon afterwards. Now, nearly all Yorkshire, with the very significant exception of Hull, lay at the King's feet.

The Walk

1. Begin at Oakwell Hall Country Park. From Warrens Lane, turn left into Nova Lane and left again at Field Head Lane. Walk up Field Head Lane, which crosses the motorway.

2. Beyond the M62, turn left onto the A650 and then right into Station Road, before bearing right into Moorside Road, marking Newcastle's centre ground.

3. At the end of Moorside Road, turn left into King Street, Drighlington, which affords spectacular views across country. The configuration of the landscape does lend credibility to Sir Thomas's claim that the Roundhead left wing was hidden from view. Beyond the traffic lights is Bradford Road, along which Gifford and Lord Fairfax beat their hasty retreat.

4. The Whitehall Road (A58) and Bradford Road crossroads also mark the position of Gifford's cavalry. Turn to the left into

Oakwalton Hall was used by Charlotte Brontë as the model for 'Fieldhead' in her novel, 'Shirley'. During the English Civil War, the hall was owned by the Batt family. After the Battle of Adwalton Moor, the Royalists burst into the building in their search for fleeing Roundheads – much to the distress of Mrs Batt, who was ill at the time.

Walk 15: Adwalton Moor 75

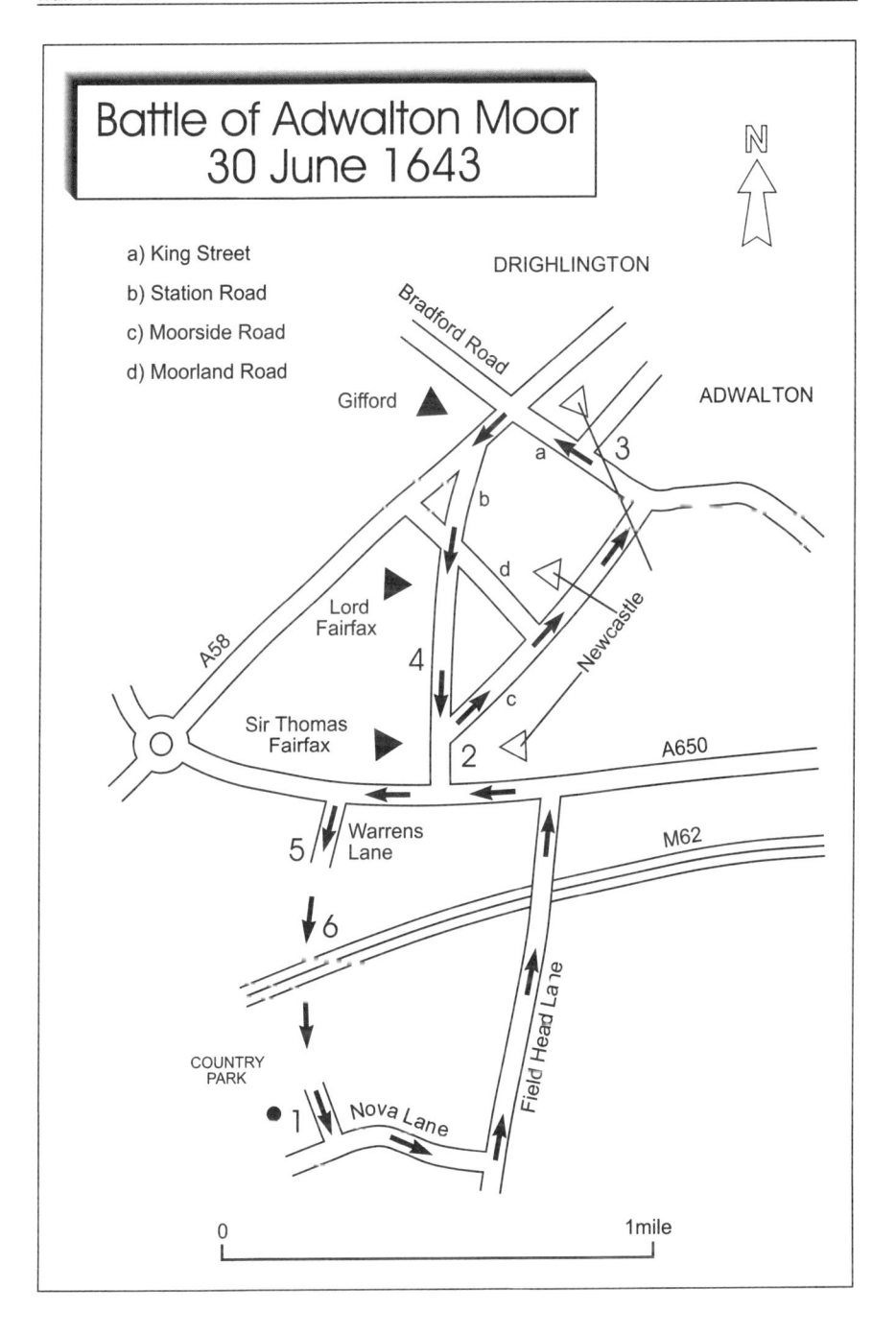

Battle of Adwalton Moor
30 June 1643

a) King Street
b) Station Road
c) Moorside Road
d) Moorland Road

Whitehall Road and left again into Station Road (B6125). In walking down Station Road, you are roughly following the line taken up by the Roundhead force. In the middle, where the land is still open common – and doubtless the scene of heavy fighting – was Lord Fairfax.

5. At the end of Station Road, turn right, onto the A650. This is a busy road, but it is bordered by a wide, well-tended grass verge. Turn left into Warrens Lane – the dusty track marked by the electricity pylon – where Sir Thomas Fairfax took up position. The track develops into the Spen Valley Heritage Trail. It was down this lane that Sir Thomas retreated, past Oakwell Hall, towards Halifax.

6. Warrens Lane develops into a footpath – the Spen Valley Heritage Trail. Follow this path under the motorway, to your starting point at the southern end of Warrens Lane, by Oakwell Hall.

Walk 16: The Siege of Hull

2 September – 12 October, 1643

Route: Hull's Old Town

Starting point: Beverley Gate, Hull. Parking available in City Centre multi-storey car parks

Length: 2 miles. Easy.

Map: Street Map of Hull

Access: Hull lies at the eastern end of the M62. (Although within the new county of Humberside, Hull has reverted to its old East Yorkshire identity as far as postal addresses are concerned.)

About the Walk

It is usually claimed that the English Civil War, between King Charles I and Parliament began with the raising of the King's standard at Nottingham, on 22 August 1642. In fact, the conflict began 4 months earlier – on 23 April – when the governor of Kingston Upon Hull, Sir John Hotham, denied Charles entry to the city.

Hull was important to Charles partly because of its role as a port, but also because it was second only to the Tower of London in terms of the size of its magazine: 120 cannon, 20,000 arms and 7,000 barrels of gunpowder. Unfortunately, the city's sympathies lay with Parliament and Sir John Hotham, Member of Parliament for Beverley, assumed control with 1,000 men.

Hull's defences were formidable. To the south lay the River Humber and to the east, the River Hull – with an open fort, 'South End', built in 1627 – beyond which lay a fortified wall which included a castle and two blockhouses. To the north and west was a moat, surmounted by four fortified gateways: Hessle Gate, Myton Gate, North Gate and Beverley Gate. Later, a fifth bastion was added midway between North Gate and Beverley Gate. It was at Beverley Gate that the King suffered his humiliating rebuff. He returned in July 1642, to besiege the city for almost three weeks. Hull's fresh water supply was cut off and an unsuccessful attempt was made to establish a naval blockade. The garrison did make some aggressive assaults on the Royalist positions, drawing some of the first blood of the Civil War and leading to the withdrawal of the Royalist forces.

Over the next twelve months, the focus of events moved away from Yorkshire, although the Royalists made slow but sure progress in securing much of the East Riding. In June 1643, Hull again took centre stage when it was learned that Sir John Hotham was about to switch allegiance to the King and turn the city over to the Royalists. His plot uncovered, Sir John fled, only to be captured and eventually executed along with his son. No sooner had the new governor, Lord Fairfax, taken up his duties than another crisis loomed in the form of the Royalist Earl of Newcastle whose victorious Northern Army of 16,000 men was advancing on Beverley, as a prelude to laying siege to Hull. Lord Fairfax's son, Sir Thomas, was forced to evacuate the town, which was afterwards plundered by Newcastle's troops.

Shortly after midnight on 2 September, the Royalists began constructing a series of earthworks to the north and east of the city. One line stretched north along the road to Beverley. A second line hugged the west bank of the River Hull and included a bridge of boats at Wilmington. A third, beginning at a point known as The Gallows only 500 metres from the city wall, was strung out to the west. Meanwhile, Hull's Roundhead garrison constructed earthworks of its own outside the walls, 'Mount Fort', beneath Hessle Gate in order to protect the West Jetty and another beyond North Gate. It was common practice for the besieged to use women in this work. It may have been perceived as a woman's job, but it is more likely that it was hoped the enemy would think twice before opening fire on women. The Royalists also commandeered all foodstuffs from the surrounding countryside and cut off the fresh water supply, as the King had done the year before. Owing to the subsequent shortage, no water could be spared for the garrison's horses, many of which expired.

In response, Lord Fairfax ordered the Humber's banks to be cut, flooding the land for two miles around. The countryside to the east was particularly badly affected, resulting in little military activity, but heavy rains and high tides ensured that the besiegers on all sides endured miserable conditions. Fortunately for the garrison, the 'back door' remained open, in terms of the arrival of men and supplies via the River Humber – two of Parliament's warships, the *Rainbow* and the *Unicorn* retaining control of the Humber and the River Hull.

Even so, the defenders did not have things all their own way. On 16 September, for instance, the northern blockhouse on the west bank of the River Hull was blown up by a Roundhead trooper who lit a match in the powder magazine. Fire was a constant hazard – especially from heated cannonballs, which constituted crude incendiary devices. Fairfax gave orders for all flammable materials to be stored in cellars and for buckets of water to be kept by doors.

The importance of the defenders' earthworks outside the walls was illustrated on 9 October when a party of Royalists managed to get between Mount Fort and the Hessle Gate bastion, which they scaled and entered. Sir John Meldrum saved the day by leading one hundred musketeers from Mount Fort to reinforce the defenders. The Royalists were driven out of the bastion and retired to their own lines.

This fright did not deter the Roundheads from launching their own sorties outside the walls. On 11 October, 1,000 musketeers made a three-pronged assault on the Gallows earthwork. The Royalists were driven back, first from the Gallows and then from a second entrenchment, but fresh troops were brought up, enabling them to regain their ground. However, in a bold move, Fairfax refused to allow the Roundheads back into the city. Thus encouraged, they renewed their attack, recapturing the Royalist positions. Although, after three hours fighting, they were forced to withdraw, they did so in an orderly fashion, taking a number of Royalist guns. (One of these, nicknamed 'Sweet Lips' after an infamous Hull prostitute, would be put to good use by the Roundheads in their own sieges of Royalist towns.) At this point, the Royalists made an all-out attack, committing 4,000 troops to an assault aimed at the West Jetty. Despite coming under extremely heavy fire, they were within a pistol-shot of their objective when the Roundheads counter-attacked and compelled them to retreat.

To add to Newcastle's misery, he received news that, earlier in the day, Royalist forces in Lincolnshire had been defeated at the Battle of Winceby. He despaired of taking Hull, winter was approaching and now, to cap it all, Parliament had established control across the Humber, in Lincolnshire. That night, he took the decision to cut his losses and withdraw immediately. The next day, with the Royalists retreating to York, the citizens of Hull emerged from their confinement and levelled all the earthworks. For many years, the day the siege was raised was observed in Hull as a day of public thanksgiving.

This statue of the poet, Andrew Marvell, stands outside Hull's Holy Trinity Church. Marvell, a prominent Parliamentarian, became MP for Hull in 1659 and was assistant to John Milton as Latin Secretary to the Council of State.

There is some disagreement as to the extent of casualties sustained during the siege, but the strength of the defences makes it unlikely that they were as high as those suffered in other sieges. The importance of the siege for Parliament lay in the fact that it had tied up a Royalist army for the latter part of the fighting season of 1643. In this respect, it would prove to be a turning point in the war.

The Walk

1. Start at Princes Quay. Here you will find an excavated portion of Beverley Gate where King Charles I's request to enter Hull was

Walk 16: The Siege of Hull

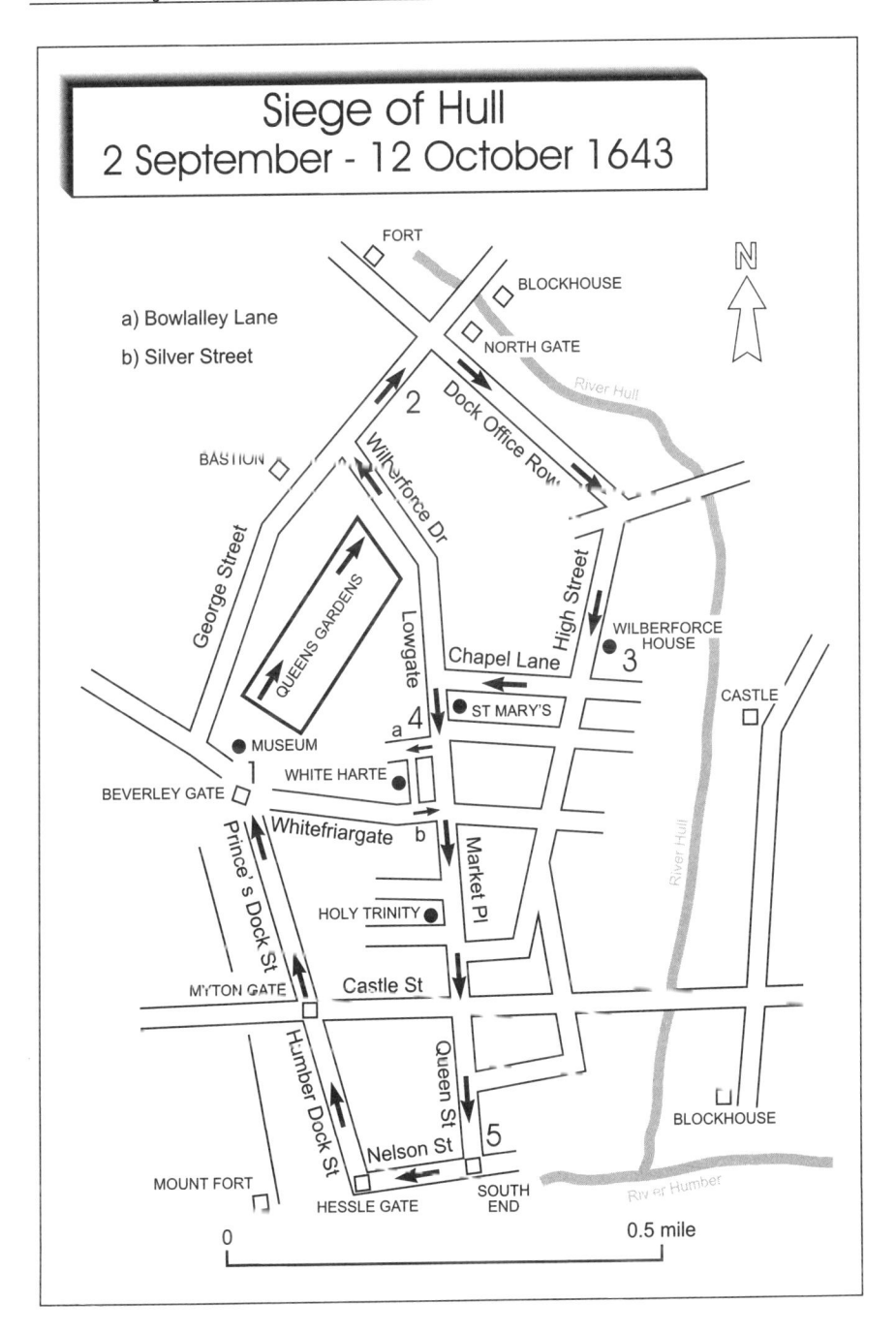

Siege of Hull
2 September - 12 October 1643

a) Bowlalley Lane
b) Silver Street

denied on 23 April 1642, the event which sparked off the English Civil War.

2. Walk over to Queens Gardens. Between 1778 and 1930, when it was filled in, this area was Queens Dock. Turn left into Wilberforce Drive, right into George Street and on to North Bridge. Just below the bridge stood North Gate and, on the opposite bank of the River Hull, the North Blockhouse.

3. Turning to the right, walk down Dock Office Row and on into High Street. On the left beyond Drypool Bridge, is Wilberforce House. Best known as the home of anti-slavery campaigner, William Wilberforce, the house once belonged to Sir John Lister, mayor of Hull, who welcomed Charles I there on the occasion of his visit in 1639.

4. Turn right into Chapel Lane and walk up to St Mary's Church in Lowgate. A little further down Lowgate to the right is Bowlalley Lane. A passage connecting Bowlalley Lane and Silver Street is the location of 'Ye Olde White Hart', the inn which contains the 'Plotting Parlour' used by Sir John Hotham to plan his initial defection to Parliament in 1642.

5. Return to Lowgate and turn right to enter Market Place. On your right is Holy Trinity Church. Cross Castle Street, proceed into Queen Street, and on to the Pier in Nelson Street, site of South End fort.

6. From the Pier, walk up Minerva Terrace and into Humber Dock Street, alongside the Marina. Cross back over Castle Street and continue up Princes Dock Street back to your starting point at Beverley Gate.

Walk 17: Battle of Selby
11 April 1644

Route: Selby Old Town

Starting Point: Selby Abbey

Length: 1 mile. Easy.

Map: Selby Street Plan

Access: Selby lies on the A63, Leeds-Hull road, 21 miles east of Leeds. Use town centre car parks.

About the Walk

In January 1644, the Marquis of Newcastle led the bulk of his Royalist army out of Yorkshire, marching north to meet the Scottish army of the Earl of Leven. The Scots were now allies of the Roundheads and it was imperative to check their advance into England. On 28 January, Colonel John Belasyse was appointed Royalist Governor of York, with the impossible brief, in Newcastle's absence, of consolidating the Royalist position in Yorkshire.

Such Royalist garrisons as remained in the East and West Ridings of Yorkshire were scattered and under-strength, and the Roundheads had little difficulty in picking them off, one by one. Belasyse decided to concentrate his overstretched resources on the West Riding and on 5 March clashed with Roundhead Colonel John Lambert outside Bradford. A determined cavalry charge put the Royalists to flight and Lambert garrisoned the town. When Belasyse returned with reinforcements on 25 March, Lambert once again put him to flight. Belasyse retreated to Selby, where he had set up his field command, and awaited developments.

Matters came to a head with the arrival in Yorkshire of Sir Thomas Fairfax – Bellasyse's Roundhead cousin – who had been engaged in a prolonged siege of Lathom House in Lancashire. Fairfax was under orders to proceed north to assist the Scots who were struggling to cope with the Marquis of Newcastle's army. However, at Ferrybridge, he fell in with his father, Lord Fairfax, and agreed to help him storm Selby – the Fairfaxes' own base until they had been driven out, to take refuge in Hull, in July 1643.

On 10 April 1644, an advance party of Roundheads encountered some Royalist horse and pursued them as far as the town, taking several prisoners. That night, Lord Fairfax quartered his army about a mile from Selby. On the following morning, he deployed his men in three divisions, one led by himself, a second led by Sir John Meldrum and a third by Lieutenant-Colonel Needham.

The plan was to attack three of the four entrances to the town – Ousegate, Gowthorpe and Brayton Lane. Although the Roundhead infantry gradually forced them to give ground, the Royalists stood firm for upwards of two hours. Eventually, however, Lord Fairfax's own division managed to force one of the defenders' barricades by Ousegate. This enabled Sir Thomas to lead his cavalry between the houses and the riverbank. His men beat off one challenge by the Royalist cavalry. A second charge was led by Belasyse himself and Sir Thomas, riding ahead of his men, was unhorsed. It was a tense moment for him, but his cavalry fought their way forward and, pressing on, drove back the Royalists – most of whom made good their escape across the Ouse by means of a bridge of boats.

Few people would describe the railway and coal mining town of Selby as particularly attractive. However, Selby's Civil War battles were fought within an old-town street pattern which has remained virtually unchanged.

The town now lay open to the Roundhead infantry. Unsupported by cavalry, their Royalist counterparts either surrendered or fled. Despite suffering heavy casualties, the Roundheads vigorously pursued those who turned tail so that, as Lord Fairfax later wrote, 'Divers slain, and lyes strewed in the way to York for four miles together.' A wounded Belasyse was taken prisoner together with 1 600 infantry, including 27 officers. Despite suffering heavy casualties, the Roundheads pursued the fleeing Royalists

The Battle of Selby is often merely a footnote in Civil War military histories, yet the action was of great significance. Parliament recognised it as such by ordering a day of public thanksgiving. The Yorkshire Royalist Sir Henry Slingsby considered the encounter 'a fatal blow to us', while Sir Thomas Fairfax remarked that it had left the Royalists in 'great distraction and fears at York'. In fact, a Roundhead siege of York was now inevitable.

The Walk

1. Begin at Selby Abbey Church. The town developed around the Abbey, begun in 1069 by a French monk, Benedict. Several abbeys – Tewkesbury, Hexham, Evesham, Byland and Selby included – have battlefield associations. During the Civil War, Selby Abbey Church suffered some damage at the hands of the Roundheads and it is said that they even used it as a stable – a tale adapted to fit many a religious establishment.

2. From the Abbey Church, walk down Park Street and turn to your left to walk up Station Road. A left turn at the top takes you into Ousegate, site of one of the Royalist barricades. This was the barricade which the Roundheads forced.

3. Walk up Ousegate to Selby Bridge. Strangely enough, there was no bridge at Selby until 1792. For two hundred years, everyone passing over it had to pay a toll. Even in 1644, the space between the houses bordering Ousegate and the River Ouse itself must have been limited and it must have been a frantic, confused encounter which took place there.

86 — Battlefield Walks in Yorkshire

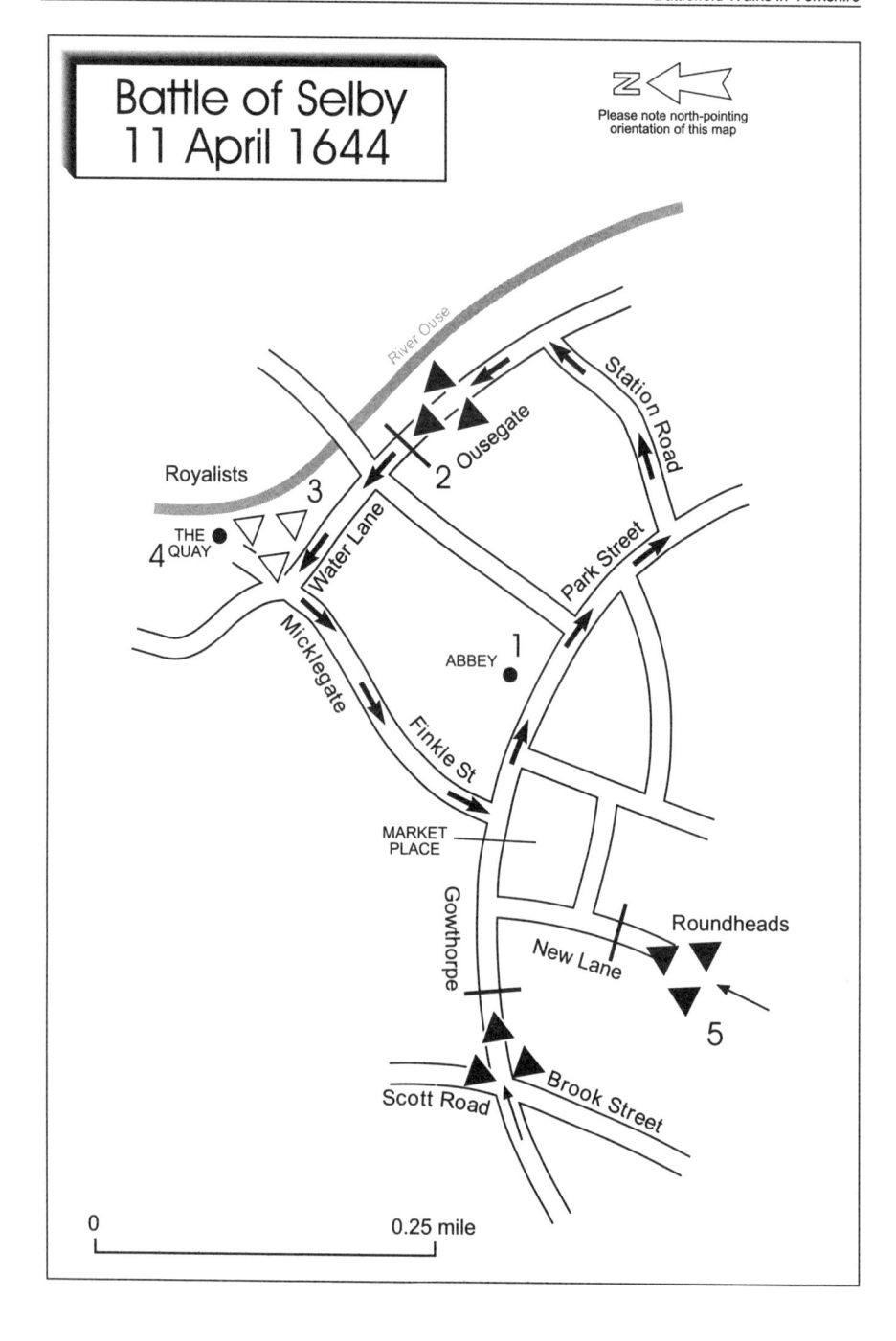

Battle of Selby
11 April 1644

Please note north-pointing orientation of this map

Royalists

THE QUAY 4

3

2 Ousegate

River Ouse

Water Lane

Micklegate

Finkle St

ABBEY 1

Station Road

Park Street

MARKET PLACE

Gowthorpe

New Lane

Roundheads

5

Scott Road

Brook Street

0   0.25 mile

4. Walk up Water Lane, at the end of which is The Quay. Before the bridge was built, passage across the water was by ferry from this point, and the Royalists' bridge of boats would have been organised here.

5. From The Quay, walk into Micklegate – the road to Cawood, along which more Royalists fled – and down into Finkle Street. This leads into Market Place, the scene of much skirmishing in the Civil War. To your right is Gowthorpe, site of the second Royalist barricade. The present-day road to Brayton (A19) runs off Gowthorpe, but the 17th-century route ran directly off Market Place, probably in the locality of New Lane – down which you may walk if, in all likelihood, you have used the car park by the supermarket.

Walk 18: Siege of York

21 April to 16 July, 1644

Route: York City Walls

Starting Point: Fishergate, York

Length: 3½ miles. Strenuous.

Map: Street Plan of York

Access: York is best approached via the A1, along the A59 turn-off from the north, or by the A64 Tadcaster road if approaching from the south. Use city centre car parks.

About the Walk

In several major cities, preparations for a probable siege during the English Civil War had been put in hand well before the event itself occurred. Royalist York was no exception. Suburbs had developed around the medieval defensive walls and, in the event of attack, the strategy was for everyone to retire within – much as folk from outlying regions had sought refuge in the past. An outer moat still existed, but it was dry in places and used mainly as a convenient dumping ground for household waste. There was deep water in the moat surrounding Clifford's Tower – the keep of the old Norman castle – but the Tower itself and much of the wall had fallen into disrepair. Remedial work was speedily undertaken. Additional new earthwork defences were constructed outside the walls, and efforts were made to build up adequate stocks of food and ammunition.

In this respect, the arsenal benefited from Queen Henrietta Maria's mission to the Netherlands. Arriving at Bridlington early in 1643 with much needed heavy artillery, the Queen's route to the Royalist capital of Oxford took her via York, where some on the munitions she had bought from the Dutch were off-loaded. With only 5,000 men – mainly infantry – under his command, the Royalist Governor of York, John Belasyse was hard pressed to hold his ground. Yet, perhaps unwisely, he had gone onto the offensive and,

Clifford's Tower is almost all that remains of York Castle. It was named after Sir Roger Clifford whose body was hung in chains on its summit after the Battle of Boroughbridge in 1322. The hub of York's defence system, Clifford's Tower was in a ruinous condition at the start of the Civil War and received a pounding from Roundhead artillery during the siege of 1644.

on 11 April 1644, the Fairfaxes had routed his force at Selby. Belasyse had been wounded and taken prisoner. York, with a skeleton garrison of only 500 men lay wide open to the Roundheads.

The Marquis of Newcastle, Royalist Commander-in-Chief of the North, was at Durham when he heard the news. Hurriedly, he marched his troops to York and, on 16 April, entered the city. Most of his 3,000 cavalry were sent on to the Midlands, while he remained with 4,000 infantry. As the Roundheads closed in, he sent a message to King Charles I, advising him that he could hold out for six weeks. Between 21 and 23 April, the Fairfaxes set up their headquarters at Heslington Hall, sealing off York from the east, from Fulford to the Red Tower. The Earl of Leven, whose army of Scots – allies of Parliament – had followed in Newcastle's wake, took responsibility for the west and south, from Fulford to Poppleton. For the time being, the way to the north remained open.

For the first few weeks of the siege, fighting was sporadic. With the appearance – on 4 June – of the Earl of Manchester for Parliament, the gap to the north was plugged. With a besieging force of 30,000 against Newcastle's 4,800, there could be no excuse for Roundhead inactivity. A battery was erected upon Lamel Hill (off the present-day Heslington Road) from which the city defences could be bombarded. As a result, Clifford's Tower suffered some damage and the approach to Walmgate came under Roundhead control. Sir Thomas Fairfax's engineers managed to mine Walmgate Bar, but the plan was discovered in time and the mines were rendered harmless. The suburbs in all directions were destroyed, most of the damage being deliberately inflicted by the garrison – a dangerous defensive ploy because the burnt-out shells of the once prosperous homes were used as cover, Roundhead snipers making full use of the facility. Only too conscious of the overwhelming strength of the investing forces, Newcastle's strategy was to play for time, in the expectation that, in the best tradition, Prince Rupert's Royalist cavalry would come galloping to the rescue. He gained a valuable week before negotiations were broken off and the Roundheads made a concerted effort to break in.

Among the weak points identified for the exercise was St Mary's Tower – which was to be mined – and The King's Manor. This may have constituted part of an overall strategy for storming the walls at several locations simultaneously, but an assault on the north-west corner was undertaken prematurely. According to some contemporary sources, a Colonel Crawford, anxious to earn the glory of taking the city, took it upon himself to spring the mines under St Mary's and storm the breach with 300 men. On 16 June, the tower was blown up and The King's Manor taken, but the small force was ultimately beaten back, sustaining heavy casualties. Considering the odds it was up against, the garrison was standing up to the siege pretty well. Although the 'spotted fever' was in evidence, many of the besiegers, particularly the Scots, had also fallen ill. Fairfax complained that he was running short of firearms and ammunition, and that his men were owed 4 months' back pay. (The cost of keeping Fairfax's army in the field was roughly £15,000 per month.) Worse still, on 30 June, Prince Rupert and 17,500 Royalists were reported to be approaching Knaresborough. In response, the Roundhead forces abandoned their siege of York and marched out to Marston Moor to await Rupert's arrival. Newcastle followed suit, to join the Prince. The fate of York would depend upon the forthcoming Battle of Marston Moor. Great was the consternation when, on the evening of 2 July, a weary procession of survivors of the beaten Royalist army appeared at Micklegate Bar.

The Roundheads were slow in following up their victory, giving Rupert time to regroup and march out of the city. When they did return, on 4 July, they gave the remnants of the garrison one final opportunity to capitulate, before mounting an all-out assault. The offer was accepted. With Rupert beaten, there could be no hope of relief. The surrender – taken on 16 July – was negotiated by Sir Thomas Fairfax, who ensured that it was honourable. The garrison was permitted to depart, unmolested and the townsfolk were left to resume their daily activities in what remained of their homes. The Siege of York, which had lasted just 5 days short of 3 months, was at an end.

The Walk

1. Begin at Fishergate Bar, climbing a flight of stone steps to a narrow walkway which will take you along the city walls in an easterly direction. It is no longer possible to walk through the bars so, on reaching Walmgate Bar, a little further along, walk down to the road to rejoin the wall on the other side. This south-east corner suffered much damage during the siege. All the houses outside the wall – stretching into present-day Lawrence Street – were destroyed and Roundhead artillery pounded Walmgate Bar to such an extent that it had to be substantially rebuilt in 1648.

2. To the left, amid modern blocks of flats, languishes St Margaret's Church. Young and fit walkers can slip down from the wall at this point, while the more staid will have to descend from the Red Tower, ahead and walk back. St Margaret's is closed and in a ruinous state, but its finely carved porch, including signs of

the zodiac, is of interest. Belonging originally to St Lawrence's Church, the porch was preserved by Sir Thomas Fairfax and afterwards removed to St Margaret's. St Lawrence's (demolished in 1881) was occupied as a forward post by Fairfax and it was from here as well as from Lamel Hill, that Walmgate Bar was shelled.

3. The Red Tower, built in 1490 as a watch tower, also suffered through bombardment. The Red Tower marks the beginning of a gap in the wall. The Tower stood at what was once the southern tip of an area of marshland known as the King's Fishpond, an expanse of water which had been formed with the damming of the River Foss in 1068, during the construction of the original York Castle. By the date of the siege, had it not been on the verge of drying up, it would have constituted an effective barrier. The outer moat, at least, from the Red Tower to Fishergate was probably full of water.

4. From the Red Tower, walk along Foss Islands Road, crossing the river by Layerthorpe Bridge, to rejoin the wall in Jewbury. A formidable postern was sited here until its demolition in 1829. To the left is St Cuthbert's Church, stranded in a sea of later development and looking as forlorn as St Margaret's. Again, St Cuthbert's was damaged by Roundhead shells, resulting in a rebuilding programme after the siege. Further along Jewbury is Merchant Taylor's Hall, one of many buildings used to provide temporary hospital facilities for the wounded.

5. At Monk Bar, descend and walk into Goodramgate, and on into Minster Yard. Although York Minster was not a military objective, it is surprising that it survived the siege relatively unscathed. Regular services, attended by up to one thousand people, were held in the Minster during the siege, and the defenders were quick to ascribe its deliverance to divine intervention. Several well-bred Royalist casualties of both the siege and the Battle of Marston Moor were buried in the Minster, while the Chapter House contains a memorial to the Fairfaxes as

Walk 18: Siege of York   93

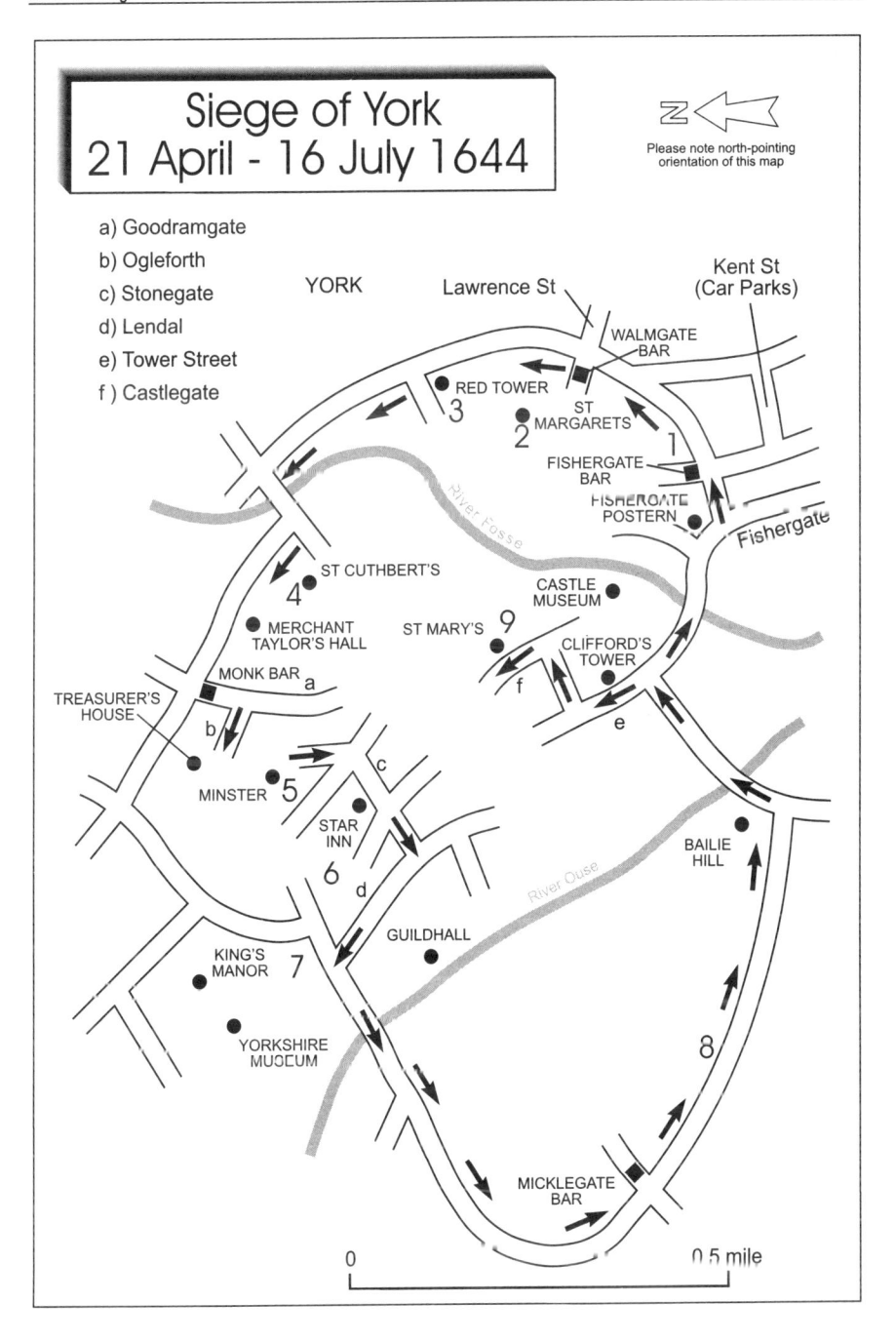

Siege of York
21 April - 16 July 1644

Please note north-pointing orientation of this map

a) Goodramgate
b) Ogleforth
c) Stonegate
d) Lendal
e) Tower Street
f) Castlegate

YORK
Lawrence St
Kent St (Car Parks)
WALMGATE BAR
RED TOWER
ST MARGARETS
FISHERGATE BAR
River Fosse
FISHERGATE POSTERN
Fishergate
ST CUTHBERT'S
CASTLE MUSEUM
MERCHANT TAYLOR'S HALL
ST MARY'S
CLIFFORD'S TOWER
MONK BAR
TREASURER'S HOUSE
MINSTER
STAR INN
River Ouse
BAILIE HILL
GUILDHALL
KING'S MANOR
YORKSHIRE MUSEUM
MICKLEGATE BAR

0   0.5 mile

a reward for using their influence to preserve the Minster from destruction after the surrender.

6. Walk out of the Minster Grounds across Petergate and into Stonegate and the bustle of the city centre – a world apart from the serenity of the walls. In Stonegate is 'Ye Olde Starr Inne', another building used as a temporary hospital facility. Its cellars are allegedly still haunted by the wounded and echo to the ghostly cries of the victims of primitive field surgery. At the end of Stonegate, on the far side of St Helen's Square, is The Guildhall. Severely damaged by an air raid in 1942, it was restored in 1960, the east window being redesigned to include a scene depicting the siege.

7. From The Guildhall, a short walk up Lendal and across Museum Street will take you into the Museum Gardens and the Yorkshire Museum, which has on display a model of the Battle of Marston Moor. In the grounds, to the rear of the Museum, is the King's Manor, residence of both the Earl of Strafford and, when he was visiting York, King Charles I. It was originally the house of the Abbot of St Mary's. Once one of the richest Benedictine Monasteries in England, the Abbey was already in a ruinous condition, having been largely destroyed during the dissolution of the monasteries. St Mary's Tower was destroyed in the attack of 16 June 1644 and the tower which now stands at the north corner of the Abbey Wall post-dates the Civil War.

8. Return to Museum Street and turn to the right, crossing the Ouse by Lendal Bridge to rejoin the wall at Lendal Tower. This section of the wall follows Station Road and Queen Street. The point where the wall turns towards Micklegate may have been the location of Sadler Tower, destroyed by artillery fire in early July 1644. It was before nearby Micklegate Bar that the beaten Royalists pleaded for admission after Marston Moor, while those inside attempted to bar the entry of anyone who had not been a member of the original garrison. Continue to Baile Hill. This is, perhaps, the most attractive portion of the walled walk. There is a steep incline to the moat and the scars of Roundhead artillery

fire can be identified along this section of wall. The tree covered mound is all that remains of the 'companion' castle to Clifford's Tower. During the siege, it was crowned with two cannons.

9. Descend from the wall at The Baile, recrossing the Ouse at Skeldergate Bridge. Clifford's Tower in Tower Street looms up on the left. Still very defensible in the mid-17th century, new floors and a gun platform were added by the Royalist garrison. To the rear of Clifford's Tower is St Mary's Church, now a heritage centre tracing the development of York, including its role in the Civil War. Several members of the garrison were buried here. From St Mary's, retrace your steps up Tower Street to reach your starting point at Fishergate.

Walk 19: Battle of Marston Moor
2 July 1644

Route: Long Marston – Marston Moor – Long Marston

Starting point: The Sun Inn, Long Marston

Length: 10 miles. Moderate.

Maps: Ordnance Survey Explorer 289 & 290

Access: Long Marston is situated on the B1224, 7 miles west of York. Roadside parking in the village.

About the Walk

The task of relieving the Roundhead Siege of York (see Walk 18) fell to Prince Rupert, who was engaged in recruitment and training in Shrewsbury. His progress to York was necessarily slow, for initially, he could call on only 8,000 men. Building up his force en route, he enjoyed some success in Lancashire subduing, in turn, Stockport, Bolton and Liverpool.

On 30 June, Rupert reached Knaresborough, just 14 miles (22.5 kilometres) from York. The Roundheads were, not unnaturally, convinced that he intended to launch an attack from this direction. Raising the siege, they marched out to Marston Moor, an expanse of heath 7 miles (11.27 kilometres) to the west of the city, to block his approach. However, instead of advancing as expected, Rupert swung north, crossing the River Ure at Boroughbridge and the River Swale at Thornton Bridge, before turning south to approach York from a totally unexpected direction. Upon his arrival in the vicinity of York, Rupert sent Lord Goring into the city to order Newcastle to be ready to march against the Roundheads at 4.00am the next day (2 July).

The allies passed an uneasy night upon the moor, pondering Rupert's next move. Afraid that he might try to slip away to join the King, they decided to block the road to the south at Selby. Accordingly, in the morning, the main body of the Roundhead army marched out, leaving 4,000 dragoons behind. When Rupert's forces began arriving on the moor, the allied column was strung out vulnerably, and a number of cavalry charges at this juncture could have wrought havoc within its ranks. However, the Prince could do nothing until reinforced by Newcastle, whose men – to Rupert's dismay – straggled in throughout the day, giving the allies sufficient time to regroup.

The Royalists were drawn up to the north of Marston Lane – the Tockwith to Long Marston road – and the combined Roundhead forces to the south. The most prominent feature of the battlefield was a ditch immediately in front of the Royalist lines. Linking Syke Beck with Atterwith Dyke, it was of varying depth and most probably dry.

Under his command, Rupert had 11,000 Foot, 6,500 Horse and sixteen pieces of artillery. His right wing, under Lord Byron, comprised 2,500 cavalry and 500 musketeers. It was almost evenly balanced by the left wing, with Lord Goring commanding 2,100 Horse and 500 musketeers. The centre comprised 10,000 infantry and was fronted by musketeers. As Commander in Chief, Rupert took charge of a small reserve.

Across the road, the Roundhead army possessed a strong numerical advantage. Sir Thomas Fairfax, on the right, with around 3,000 men, faced Goring. Cromwell and some 4,000 men on the left, were drawn up against Byron. Exact deployment in numerical terms, is unclear, but it is likely that the combined English and Scottish infantry in the centre amounted to some 20,000 men. A total of twenty-five guns were ranged across Marston Hill.

Preliminary manoeuvres having taken up the best part of the day – it was now approaching 7.00pm – Newcastle asked Rupert whether he intended to give battle that night. The Prince replied that the following morning would be soon enough and went off to his supper. Newcastle got into his coach to smoke a pipe.

In the allied lines, there was no such laxness. As soon as they perceived the Royalists standing down, the Roundheads began to move forward. It was Cromwell who made the first contact. Possibly, the ditch separating the two sides had been filled in at its western extremity, giving Cromwell a clear run. Byron advanced to meet

Cromwell, but his men became bogged down in marshy ground. In an attempt to bolster Byron's crumbling line, Rupert left his command post, arriving on the scene with his own Lifeguard. Cromwell, who may have been supported by Leslie, eventually broke through, sending the Royalist right wing – Rupert's own men included – reeling back towards Wilstrop Wood.

The Earl of Manchester's infantry division on the left was also making good progress but, on the right wing, Sir Thomas Fairfax had come to grief. He experienced difficulty negotiating the ditch and suffered heavy casualties. His brother, Charles, was killed and he himself was wounded in the face. When a portion of Goring's cavalry was put to flight, Fairfax's men pursued them off the field and Sir Thomas found himself alone, surrounded by Royalists. By the expedient of removing from his hat the 'Signal' identifying him as a Roundhead officer, he contrived to slip through and regain the safety of his own lines.

Most of Goring's cavalry remained intact and charged, scattering Fairfax's second line and continuing on to attack the Roundhead baggage train. More of Goring's cavalry fell upon the infantry of the

The imposing monument to the Battle of Marston Moor was erected in 1936 by the Cromwell Association and the Harrogate group of the Yorkshire Archaeological Society. A newly constructed (2002) lay-by opposite the monument provides car parking and an alternative starting point for the walk.

Roundhead centre right. Additional pressure from Newcastle's famous 'Whitecoats' proved too much for them and they turned tail. So desperate did the situation seem that even The Earl of Leven and Lord Fairfax joined in the flight. Leven made for Leeds, while Fairfax fled all the way to his home, near Cawood and, according to his enemies, immediately went to bed.

Meanwhile, on the Roundhead left wing, Cromwell had been absent from the field. Having sustained a minor neck wound, he had retired to a cottage in Tockwith to have it dressed, but he was soon back in the saddle. Now, he led his regiment around to the rear of the Royalist lines to challenge Goring's cavalry, which was taken completely by surprise. The latter had considered the battle won and now, seemingly out of nowhere, appeared a strong, disciplined body of enemy Horse. Confused and in disarray, they scattered, relieving the pressure on the hardcore of the Scots' division on the centre right which had stood its ground. What had appeared to be a famous Royalist victory had quickly developed into a Royalist rout.

Cromwell next turned his attention to the 'Whitecoats', who were soon beset from all sides. In part, to preserve their honour as well as to cover the Royalist retreat, they refused all offers of quarter and fought almost to the last man. When it was all over, Royalist dead totalled 4,000, while the Roundheads lost perhaps as few as 300. It is said that Prince Rupert evaded capture by hiding in a beanfield. Nevertheless, while his fellow commanders wallowed in the misery of defeat, Rupert eventually rallied the remains of his army – 6,000 men – and marched back across the Pennines. Although the north was lost, there was still life and hope in the south and west.

The Walk

1. I usually begin – and conclude – this walk at the Sun Inn at the corner of Marston Lane in the village of Long Marston. From this starting point, proceed along Marston Lane towards Tockwith. On the right-hand side of the road, a short distance from the junction with the B1224 is Marston Hall – allegedly haunted by the ghost of Cromwell who is said to have slept here before the battle.

2. It is easy to see how Long Marston acquired its name, for houses straggle along Marston Lane to its meeting with Atterwith Lane. Opposite Atterwith Lane is a track leading to Cromwell Gap, the escape route taken by Goring's fleeing cavalry. Also clearly visible to the left is Cromwell Plump, the high point of the local landscape, the ridge identifying the preliminary Roundhead positions, to the rear of which was the baggage train.

3. Continue to the battlefield monument, situated at the corner of a track known locally as Moor Lane. To the rear of the memorial, erected by the Cromwell Association, is a descriptive battle plan, while the memorial inscription states – quite firmly – that 'the Parliamentary army, left to the leadership of Oliver Cromwell supported by David Leslie completed the defeat of the forces of Prince Rupert'.

4. Continue walking towards Tockwith, turning right into Kendal Lane – a portion of the Jorvik Way – marking Cromwell's position. Walk on until you reach the public footpath sign on the right. Follow this path, which involves negotiating some simple stiles, which takes you to the rear of the spot occupied by Rupert's cavalry and the Royalist centre right.

5. Instead of traversing the battlefield to link up with Moor Lane the footpath veers to the north-east, towards Wilstrop Wood. On the western flank of the wood is the site of the beanfield where Rupert sought refuge. The path continues along the southern rim of the wood, at the far corner of which there once stood a gate – the focus of yet another of the many stories which have often been told about the battle. When Rupert's cavalry was in full retreat, a young girl attempted to facilitate their escape by opening this gate. However, the fleeing Royalists, while taking full advantage of her forethought, trampled her underfoot, leaving in their wake a poor mangled corpse.

6. From this point, take the farm track which opens up on your right. Continue along the track, turning right at the end and, a little further along, right again at White Sike Bridge on to Atterwith Lane. Turn right into Marston Lane and make your

Walk 19: Battle of Marston Moor 101

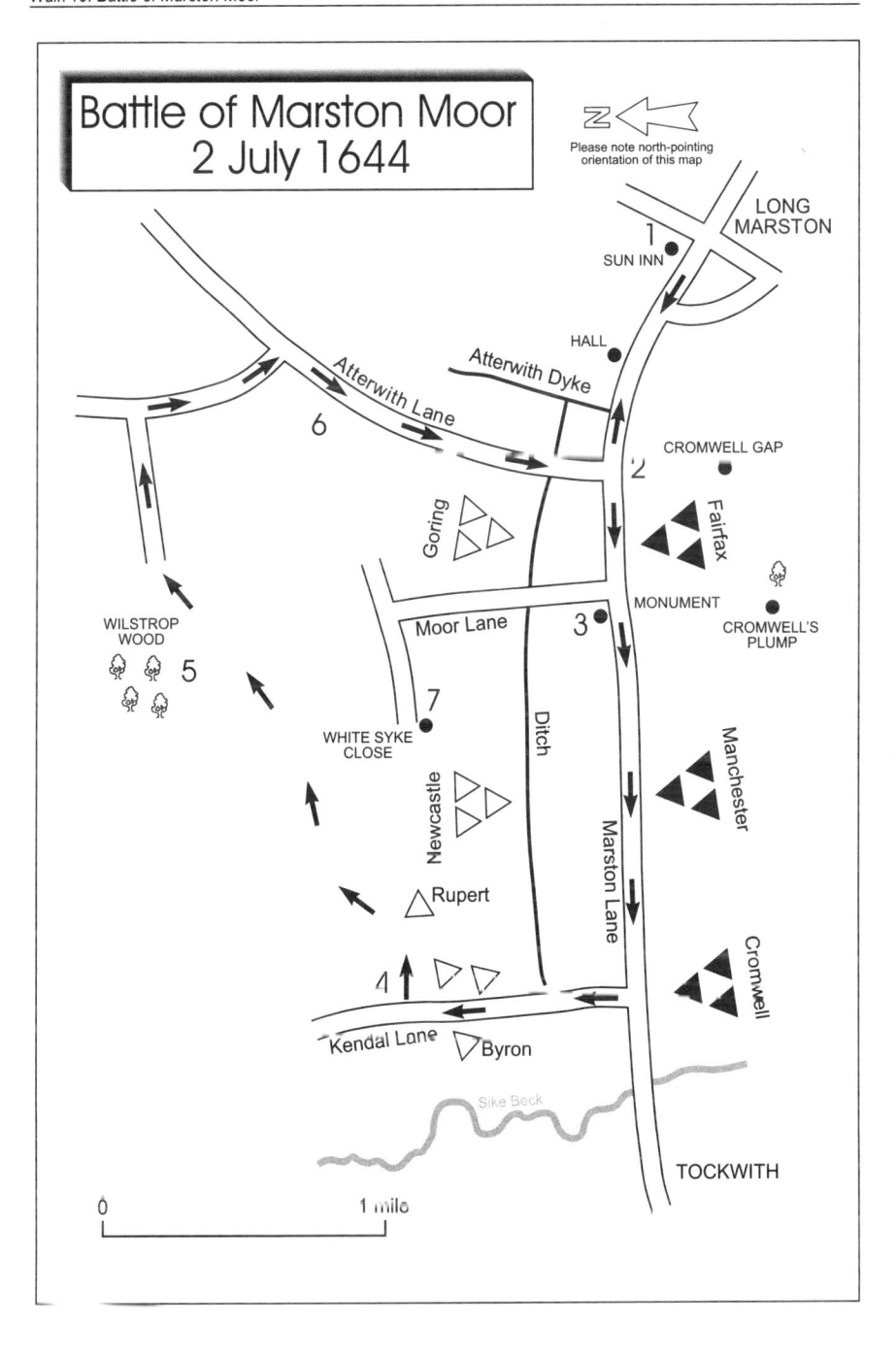

way back to the monument. Goring's cavalry were drawn up across Atterwith Lane and many relics – cannon balls, bullets, sword-blades – have been unearthed along here.

7. Before returning to your starting point in Long Marston, proceed up Moor Lane, beside the monument. The line of the ditch, in front of the Royalist positions can still be made out. Where the track forks, turn to the left and continue walking. The field where the track terminates is White Syke Close where Newcastle's Whitecoats were annihilated, and where they lie buried. Moor Lane is said to be haunted by the ghosts of exhausted combatants, wending their weary way from the battlefield, and it is not a spot where impressionable folk would care to linger in the failing light of day.

Walk 20: Siege of Scarborough Castle
18 February – 25 July, 1645

Route: Scarborough Old Town

Starting Point: Corner of Newborough and North Street.

Length: 2 miles. Strenuous.

Map: Scarborough Street Plan

Access: Scarborough occupies a prominent position on the North Yorkshire coastline 41 miles to the north east of York and 42 miles to the north of Hull. Use one of the town centre car parks but, to avoid congestion, try to visit in early spring or autumn.

About the Walk

Established in the twelfth century, Scarborough Castle was, by 1540, in an advanced state of disrepair. Yet, the site's magnificent defensive qualities had been recognised since the Bronze Age and the castle itself, despite its condition, could still be of great value to its masters.

In the event, at the outset of the Civil War, Scarborough was quickly claimed for Parliament by one of its two MPs, Sir Hugh Cholmley. He arrived in September 1642 and set about strengthening the defences. In the town, he built a new gate at Auborough Bar and a new gate and wall at Newborough Bar. The town ditch was deepened at St Nicholas Gate and a new ditch excavated at Ramsdale. In addition to renovation work within the castle, he constructed two batteries – South Steel battery at the eastern extremity of the castle dyke, and Bushell's battery to the west, in front of the castle barbican.

On 20 March 1643, Cholmley held a secret meeting with Queen Henrietta Maria, at York. On his return to Scarborough, he announced that he had decided to change sides and hold the town for the Royalists. Cholmley was extremely popular among Scarborians and the vast majority went along with his change of

Few castle ruins constitute a more impressive site than those of Scarborough Castle. It was never taken by force, despite being besieged six times in its colourful history.

heart. Parliament charged him with high treason and despatched Sir John Hotham from Hull to re-take Scarborough. Hotham – Cholmley's cousin and soon to become a turncoat himself – was ambushed at Ramshill and forced to withdraw.

For the next two years, Parliament left Cholmley alone, even though he proved a thorn in its side, mounting raids throughout the East Riding. At length, with Royalist fortunes in sharp decline, Parliament's attention turned to the last remaining Royalist strongholds in the north.

At the beginning of 1645, Scarborough was the only North Sea port of any value left to the Royalists. As long as it continued to function, stores could be imported, and it became a priority target for Roundhead forces. Cholmley prepared for a siege.

On 18 February 1645, Sir John Meldrum's Roundheads attacked and overran the town, capturing 32 guns, the harbour and 120 ships. Lacking the firepower necessary for breaching the walls, Meldrum did not follow up his advantage by storming the castle – to which Cholmley had retreated to save the town from destruction. Meldrum did take the South Steel battery, but was unable to make any impression on Bushell's battery. Accordingly, he dug in and ordered up some heavy guns. By sea, from Hull came a powerful long-cannon - a 'demi-culverin' called 'Sweet Lips', captured during the unsuccessful Royalist siege of Hull. By road, from York, came the biggest cannon in the country, the 'Cannon Royal'. Weighing over three tons, it could fire balls of more than sixty pounds. Meldrum had it dragged into St Mary's Church and mounted in the chancel, from which point it could be fired at the castle keep.

Meldrum spent some time in attempting to encourage Cholmley to give in. He wrote letters to Cholmley and his officers and shot messages attached to arrows into the castle yard, hoping to persuade the troopers to surrender. (One wonders whether any casualties resulted from these missiles.) By the middle of March, the Roundhead guns were in place and Meldrum was ready to commence his assault. However, one day, while supervising final arrangements, he fell off the cliff. It took him six weeks to recover. Cholmley used the opportunity to attack the South Steel battery, claiming that his men killed or wounded two hundred of the enemy.

With Meldrum's recovery, the Roundhead guns began to batter the castle keep. Although the walls were fifteen feet thick, the 'Cannon Royal' was firing at a distance of only two hundred yards. After three days of continuous pounding, the west wall collapsed. Once again, if Meldrum had taken the initiative and stormed the breach, all would have been over. Instead, he sent Cholmley another demand to surrender. Instead of surrendering, Cholmley reinforced the castle gatehouse with the stones from the collapsed wall. When Meldrum did finally attack, he took Bushell's battery, but was unable to proceed any further. With some satisfaction, Cholmley noted that the stones also made excellent ammunition to hurl down upon the heads of the attackers.

With artillery operating from St Mary's and Bushell's battery, the Roundheads slowly but surely reduced the castle to rubble. On 10 May, a Colonel Compton led a successful Royalist sortie against Bushell's, destroying the guns mounted there. The following day saw some of the bloodiest fighting of the siege, in and around the castle barbican. As the Roundheads were gaining the upper hand,

Meldrum was hit by a musket ball and his men withdrew. He had been mortally wounded and died a few days later.

Meldrum's successor, Sir Matthew Boynton, was of the opinion that enough Roundhead blood had been spilt in efforts to storm the castle. Instead, he continued the cannonade, supported by an additional battery at Peasholm and warships stationed off the headland. Cholmley struggled on for several more weeks. In the end, he was beaten by dwindling stocks of gunpowder, a shortage of water and, most of all, by scurvy. The dread disease had killed or incapacitated half the garrison. Yet, despite his untenable situation, Cholmley still contrived to negotiate generous terms for the surrender. The garrison was given permission to march to the nearest Royalist stronghold. He himself – penniless – boarded a ship bound for Holland. Like many others, he had served the king faithfully, beggaring himself in the process. The reduction of Scarborough Castle had also cost Parliament dear, entailing the use of some 2,000 troops, 16 ships and the most powerful ordnance in the country.

The Walk

1. Begin at the corner of Newborough and North Street, approximately the position of Newborough Bar, the main entrance to the old town. Walk up North Street, bearing to the right, along St Thomas Walk. To the left ran the town ditch. Continue into Castle Road and on to Auborough Street. At the junction with Auborough Street stood Oldborough Bar.

2. Continue walking up Castle Road until you reach St Mary's Church. Restoration work was undertaken in 1669 and in 1848, but the remains of the old tower, which collapsed in 1669 because of damage sustained during the siege, may still be seen.

3. A little further along, on the left, is the site of the Charnel Chapel. Formerly housing a grammar school, it had been pressed into service as a guardhouse and a forward post from which to assault Bushell's battery. Repaired in 1647, it was destroyed during the Second Civil War in 1648.

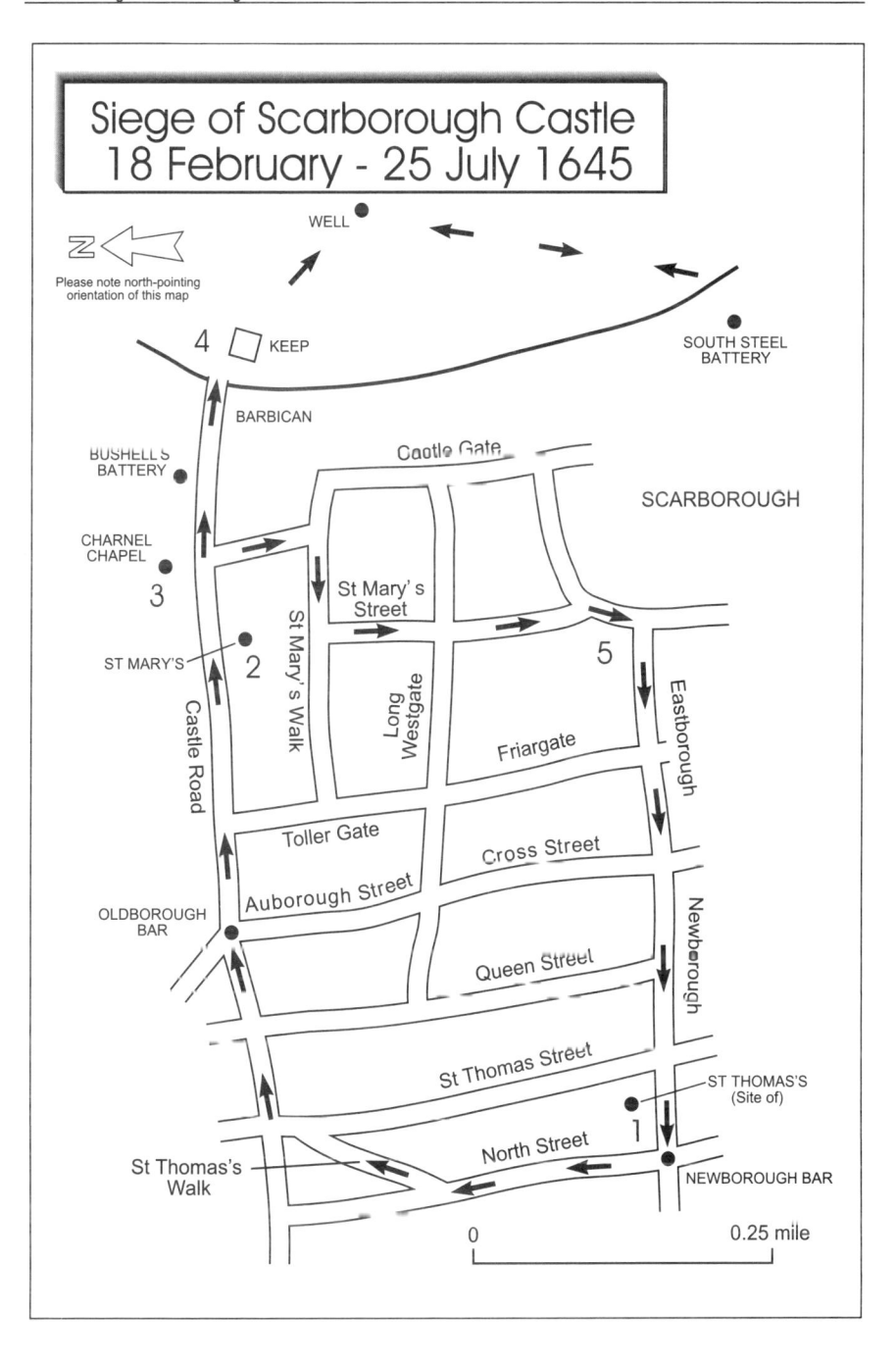

Walk 20: Siege of Scarborough Castle 107

Siege of Scarborough Castle
18 February - 25 July 1645

Please note north-pointing orientation of this map

- WELL
- 4 KEEP
- SOUTH STEEL BATTERY
- BARBICAN
- BUSHELL'S BATTERY
- Castle Gate
- SCARBOROUGH
- CHARNEL CHAPEL
- 3
- St Mary's Street
- ST MARY'S
- 2
- St Mary's Walk
- Long Westgate
- 5
- Eastborough
- Friargate
- Castle Road
- Toller Gate
- Cross Street
- Auborough Street
- Newborough
- OLDBOROUGH BAR
- Queen Street
- St Thomas Street
- ST THOMAS'S (Site of)
- 1
- St Thomas's Walk
- North Street
- NEWBOROUGH BAR

0   0.25 mile

4. Walk up to the Castle. Bushell's battery stood before the Barbican – the scene of desperate fighting. The Castle itself is in the care of English Heritage, with a range of facilities which include an audio tour. A sally port and flight of steps leading to South Steel battery have survived. From the castle, it can be seen that the old town, occupying a promontory and with cliffs on three sides, might have been defended. Once confined to the castle, however, Cholmley was effectively imprisoned. Towards the end of the siege, the only fresh water supply left to the defenders came from Our Lady's Well – and even this was running dry.

5. From the castle, descend into Castle Road. Turn left before St Mary's Church and turn right, then left again into St Mary's Street. Continue into Eastborough and walk on into Newborough. Near your starting point, beyond St Thomas Street, on the right, stood St Thomas's Church. Already in poor condition when the siege began, it was used by Meldrum as stabling and as a powder magazine. Eventually demolished, some of its lead, timber and stone were used in the restoration of St Mary's.

Walk 21: Siege of Pontefract
3 June, 1648 – 23 March, 1649

Route: Pontefract Old Town

Starting Point: Pontefract Castle Car Park

Length: 1½ miles. Strenuous.

Map: Pontefract Street Plan

Access: Pontefract is adjacent to the A1, 14 miles to the north of Doncaster. It may also be approached via the M62, Junction 32 or 33.

About the Walk

Exactly two years after the end of the English Civil War, a new conflict – often referred to as the Second Civil War – broke out. In fact, it was more of an assortment of loosely connected localised uprisings than a major contest. In May 1648, diehard Royalist factions, as far apart as Pembroke and Kent, rose up against Roundhead rule. Far more serious, however, was a threat posed by Scotland. Late allies of Parliament, the Scots were sorely disappointed at Parliament's refusal to establish Presbyterianism south of the border, and entered into an alliance with the recently deposed Charles I, who was ready to agree to anything in return for their support. It soon became common knowledge that the Marquis of Hamilton, with the support of the veteran English Cavalier, Sir Marmaduke Langdale, was planning to invade England.

Such reports fuelled thoughts of rebellion – particularly in the Yorkshire town of Pontefract, where a party of Royalists under the command of John Morris, plotted to capture the castle. Built in the 11th century, Pontefract Castle had long enjoyed the reputation of impregnability, its defences having been continuously updated to meet the requirements of successive periods. Royalist garrisons had been besieged twice during 1644-45.

Morris had seen active service at a number of sieges and at the Battle of Nantwich in 1644. Yet, he planned a bloodless coup, for he

Pontefract Castle was the last Royalist stronghold in England to fall. The citizens of Pontefract subsequently petitioned Parliament for permission to demolish the castle, and the structure – once the largest and strongest fortress in the country – was reduced to rubble. The remains of the Great Round Tower survive.

had confederates on the inside, one of whom was a corporal who promised to turn a blind eye during guard duty while Morris and 80 Royalists put up some scaling ladders against the castle walls. Unfortunately, at the time agreed upon, the corporal was the worse for drink and a less sympathetic colleague caught Morris in the act. The ladders fell into the castle's formidable ditch and the Royalists took to their heels.

In view of this scare, it was decided to strengthen Pontefract's Roundhead garrison, which numbered about 30 men and some additional troops billeted in the town. In readiness, the Governor, Colonel Overton, requisitioned supplies, including a number of beds. On 3 June 1648, some carts bearing the beds arrived at the castle – accompanied by Morris and some of his men, disguised in 'civvies'. Despite being even more farcical than the first scheme, this one actually worked. Morris sent away the sentries with money to purchase ale for themselves. He entered the castle, overpowered the rest of the guards and the Governor, who were all thrown into the dungeons, 35 feet below ground.

Morris was given the rank of Colonel and ushered in as the Royalist Governor. He found the castle well provisioned with food and ammunition but, as his adherents very soon rose to over 1,000, he laid in additional supplies by mounting several raids in the countryside. It was just as well because the castle was very soon besieged by 5,000 government regulars, commanded by Sir Edward Rhodes and Sir Henry Cholmley, brother of Sir Hugh who had held Scarborough Castle for the Royalists.

It must have been a bitter disappointment to Morris when, on 16 August 1648, Oliver Cromwell routed the army of Hamilton and Langdale at the Battle of Preston. It was rumoured that Langdale, who had been taken to Nottingham, was subsequently to be removed to Pontefract and executed in full view of the garrison if it refused to surrender. Morris devised a daring plan to secure Langdale's release.

On the evening of 28 October, a small detachment of horse slipped out of the castle and headed for Doncaster, twelve miles away. The aim was to capture the Roundhead Colonel Thomas Rainsborough, who was quartered in the town, and exchange him for Langdale at a later date. The plan miscarried and Rainsborough was killed, although the Royalists did return safely to Pontefract, with 50 prisoners in tow – which, in itself, suggests that the siege was still not watertight. In fact, one of the castle gates was kept open, being covered by a small garrison stationed in a house called 'New Hall', about a musket shot from the walls.

On 13 November, one of Cromwell's best commanders, Major-General John Lambert, arrived on the scene. Lambert thought Pontefract an 'unlucky hole'. Cromwell, who also spent some weeks there, observed that the castle was 'very well known to be one of the strongest inland Garrisons of the Kingdom.' Lambert pounded the walls with heavy mortars and mounted some assaults, during which many of his men were killed with rocks hurled from above. Yet, in the final analysis, all he could do was to wait.

While the king lived, Morris felt there was still hope for the Royalist cause. Even after the catastrophe of Charles's execution on 30 January 1649, he continued to hold out, proclaiming as king the Prince of Wales. The first money coined in England bearing the name of Charles II was coined at Pontefract by Morris. Even so, the end was inevitable. By March 1649, provisions were running low and disease was taking its toll. Morris had refused offers of £2,000 to deliver the castle up to Parliament, but when Lambert had leaflets thrown over the castle walls, offering honourable conditions for capitulation, he accepted.

The offer did contain some small print, to the effect that quarter would not be extended to six persons, who would not be named until after the articles of surrender had been signed. The exceptions were to be two men charged with the murder of Colonel Rainsborough, three conspirators who had been Morris's correspondents inside the castle prior to its seizure, and Morris himself. On 22 March 1649, Lambert took the surrender, bringing the Second Civil War to a close. One of Rainsborough's killers escaped; the other, in company with Morris, was executed at York.

Infuriated at the trouble it had caused him, Cromwell ordered Pontefract Town Council to petition Parliament to have the castle demolished. Having been exploited by successive garrisons for almost a decade, the townsfolk were pleased to oblige, and so it was reduced to the sad ruin which we see today.

The Walk

1. Begin at Pontefract Castle car park. The castle – well signposted – is approached from South Baileygate (A645). At the traffic lights, turn up North Baileygate and take the first left just before Beech Hill. The (free) car park is on the left.

2. From the car park, turn left to walk along Castle Garth (pedestrianised) to the castle. To the left are views of the Baghill area, site of Major-General John Lambert's breastwork, covering the main gate. The present-day entrance to the castle is near Spink Lane. When I first visited the castle in 1962, it was quite a desolate spot. Much excavation and conservation work has been undertaken in the intervening years, and now there is a Visitor Centre and a wealth of information to help you find your way around the site. The walk is described as strenuous in case you wish to climb to the top of the Keep or take a trip down to the dungeons (site attendant's permission required) where Governor Overton was confined by Colonel Morris.

Walk 21: Siege of Pontefract 113

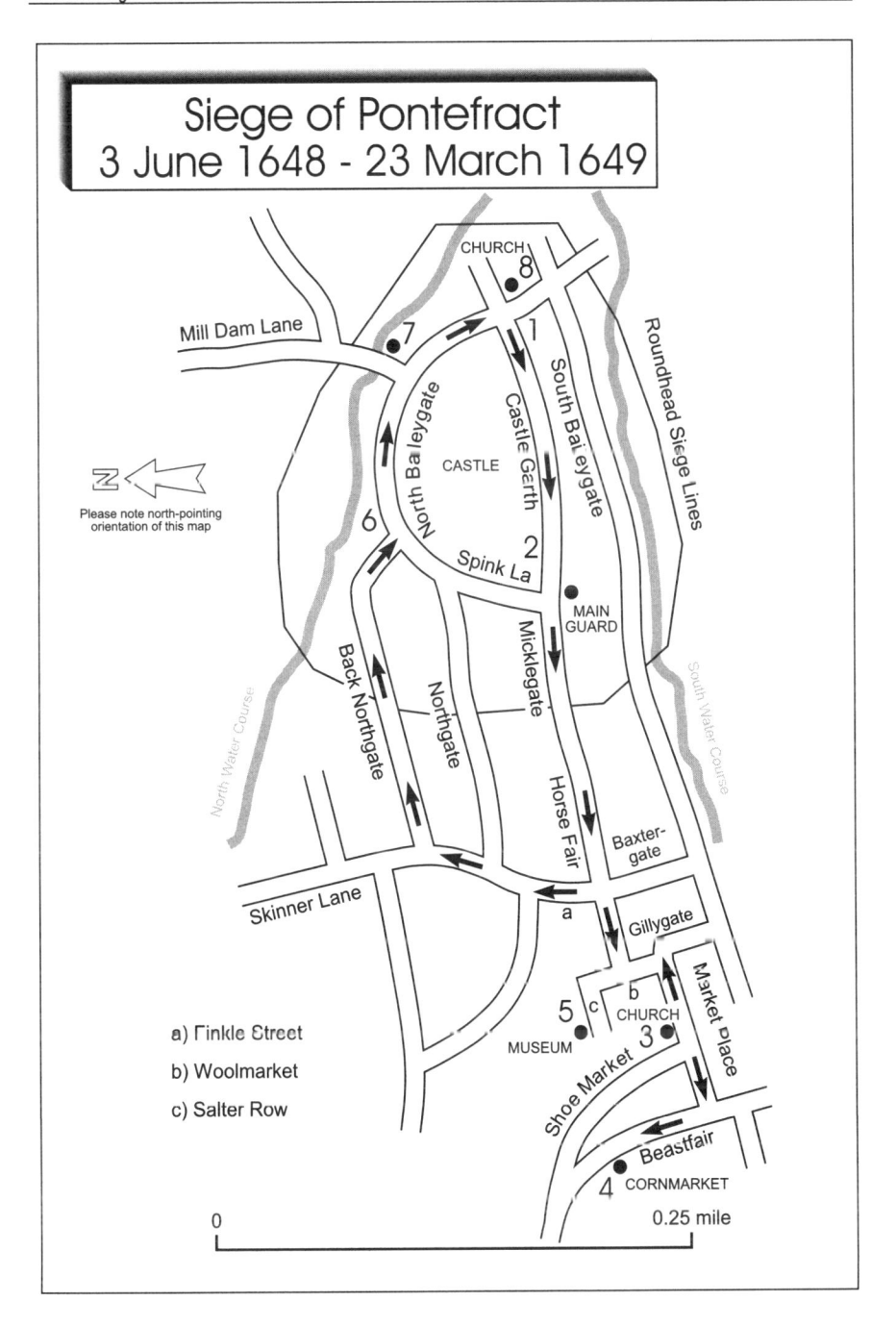

Siege of Pontefract
3 June 1648 - 23 March 1649

a) Finkle Street
b) Woolmarket
c) Salter Row

3. From the Castle, walk down Castle Garth. On your left – unmistakably – is the Main Guard, which continued in use after 1649 as a prison. Continue walking into Micklegate, on into Horse Fair and into Market Place. Here is St Giles Church which, after the Civil War damage sustained to All Saints (which you will encounter later), became Pontefract's main place of worship.

4. Walk round into Beastfair to view The Cornmarket. Behind the frontage is a house owned by one of Pontefract's leading families during the Civil Wars, the Frankes. As Roundhead sympathisers, their position during Morris's tenure cannot have been without its difficulties.

5. Retrace your steps into Market Place, turn into Woolmarket and then Salter Row to visit the town museum which holds much of relevance to the Civil War period. As you will have noted, Pontefract's street plan is quite complicated, but the signposts are extremely helpful.

6. Walk back towards Horse Fair and turn to the left into Finkle Street. Take a right turn into Back Northgate, walk on into The Butts and North Baileygate. Cromwell's breastwork stood above here.

7. As well as a rough plan of the siege works, the sketch map includes two addition vanished features – the watercourses which flanked Pontefract to north and south. Fragments of these survive in a cannibalised form. By turning into Mill Dam Lane, you can gain an idea of the direction of the north water course from viewing the ditch on the right. The eastern side of the castle was the weakest in terms of siege works.

8. Walk down North Baileygate and back to your starting point. On your left is All Saints Church, which suffered severe damage in the siege of 1645. The Royalist garrison used the tower as a vantage point, but were driven back into the castle when the Roundheads subjected the church to heavy bombardment. Within comparatively recent years, it has been restored and extended.

Walk 22: RAF Marston Moor
1941-45
Route: Tockwith – Airfield – Tockwith

Starting Point: Church of the Epiphany, Tockwith. On-road parking by the church.

Length: 5 miles. Easy.

Maps: Ordnance Survey Explorer 289

Access: Tockwith lies 7.5 miles to the west of York and can be approached from York via the B1224 or from the A1, also via the B1224.

About the Walk

On the brink of the Second World War, government surveying teams were scouring the Yorkshire landscape for sites suitable for development as military airfields. They identified as promising an area immediately to the west of York. Between York and the village of Long Marston, the countryside was undulating, but beyond Long Marston, in the vicinity of Tockwith, it levelled out to a degree which led the surveyors to earmark the location.

The proposed site was approved for heavy bomber use and the construction contract awarded to Laings. There were three standard concrete runways – the main runway 6,000 feet in length and two subsidiaries of 200 feet each. The site sprawled over the farmland to the south of the Tockwith to Cowthorpe road – a distance of two and a half miles (4 kilometres). The main aerodrome site included six hangars of the T2 type – mass-produced structures 240 feet in length and 115 feet in width, each providing 32 aircraft bays. Bordering the airfield perimeter road, between the hangars and the main runway, was the control tower – the eyes and ears of the airfield. This was a two storey structure with an interior stairway to the rear, a popular design called type 518/40.

When operating at capacity, it was anticipated that Marston Moor would be densely populated, with 206 Officers, 744 Senior NCOs and 1,164 Ratings. In addition, there would be 12 WAAF Officers, 20 SNCO WAAFs and 326 WAAF Ratings. The projected grand total of 2 472 military personnel would easily dwarf the combined population of the surrounding villages. In addition to living accommodation, dining halls and mess facilities, this self-sufficient community would have its own squash court and gymnasium, a grocery store and barbers', shoemakers' and tailors' shops. In this way, at a cost of around £500,000, many such rural landscapes were transformed during the early war years.

RAF Marston Moor opened for business on 11 November 1941, as a heavy bomber training station within Bomber Command's No 4 Group. A Training Station Commander had one of the hardest tasks in the air force. Not only was he responsible for moulding rookie air crews into shape, but he witnessed the deaths of many of them in what were often simple accidents on take-off and landing. Marston Moor lost over 60 aircraft in this way – including four which were destroyed in collisions on the ground.

Part of the airfield site is now an industrial estate. Instead of demolishing the wartime buildings, the designers have tastefully blended the old with the new. The main entrance to the airfield is now the entrance to the industrial estate. Much of the airfield architecture – including the water tower – has been preserved.

There was also some serious action, with Marston Moor supplying several bombers for the first of the '1,000 bomber' raids on Germany. On the night of 30/31 May 1942, 1,047 aircraft were despatched from British airfields to bomb Cologne. The attacking force lost 41 bombers, one of which was a Halifax based at Marston Moor. Two more were lost during the second 'Thousand Force' raid on Essen on the night of 1/2 June 1942.

The Halifax aircraft based at Marston Moor were not always to the pilots' liking. Many were past their best, having seen their share of action before being sent to Marston Moor. Even experienced pilots sometimes found them difficult to handle, as against the much lighter Wellingtons, Blenheims and Hampdens with which they were familiar. With its heavy bomb load – 13,000 lbs – a Halifax flying into the heart of Germany often had very little fuel to spare on the return journey. Valuable advice on the subject of economical cruising heights was provided by Group Captain Leonard Cheshire, who spent five months as Marston Moor's Station Commander in 1943. Cheshire also noticed that the failure of one of its four engines could send a Halifax spinning out of control, attributing the phenomenon to a rudder design fault. Cheshire's thinking in this respect was subsequently shown to be correct, although it infuriated the manufacturers.

As well as the Halifax, fighter aircraft – Spitfires and Hurricanes – were housed at Marston Moor from time to time. The concept of fighter escorts for bombers had for long been disregarded and it took repeated heavy losses for Bomber Command to admit that some measure of protection was needed against the deadly German Me109s.

During the immediate post-war months, Marston Moor remained operational and aircraft continued to arrive. The station finally closed in November 1945. For Marston Moor and many bases like it, the future was uncertain. The ex-Station Commander, Cheshire, had plans to develop the facilities along the lines of 'model' villages, providing homes and employment for ex-servicemen, a worthy scheme which never materialised. Until 1988, the Home Office used the Marston Moor hangars for storage. Today, they are still used for storage by private businesses. Some of the land has gradually reverted to agricultural usage, while part of the runway system has been utilised for specialist driver training.

The Walk

1. Begin in Tockwith at the Church of the Epiphany. Walk out of the village along the Cowthorpe road. The main aerodrome site soon looms up on the left. Continue walking and turn right into Blind Lane.

2. A little way up Blind Lane on the left are the remains of WAAF Site No 2 – now converted to light industrial use. Of greater interest, because it is rather more intact, is WAAF Site No 1, further along on the right hand side of the lane. A good overall view of the site can be obtained by looking across the fields from the lane as you approach. The most prominent feature of the scene today is a modern dwelling. The first hut you see, bordering the road, served as the picket post and detention room. At the other side of the site entrance is the well-preserved WAAF Officers' Mess. Both buildings are of the Type B variety – timber-framed with a limited projected life span. Yet, despite sixty years of neglect, many such 'temporary' edifices remain.

3. Return to the main road and turn right into Fleet Lane. Immediately opposite, dominating the local landscape, are two fine examples of T2 Hangars. Keep to the grass verge nearest the hangars. A footpath is available for a part of the route further along the road. (Concrete footpaths often border airfields.) Continue over the crossroads and turn left into Moorside. On the left are the remains of Communal Site No 1. Within recent years, some damage has been effected by the adaptation of the site to warehousing, although as you progress towards the farm, you will find the complex less disturbed.

4. Just beyond Moor Side Farm, the track veers to the left, over Ainstey Beck. A straight walk brings you to the Rudgate Roman road. Turn to the left here and walk up to the main airfield entrance, clearly indicated by the surviving water tower. In company with many main airfield sites, it has been converted to industrial usage. It is not often, however, that you meet with a site where efforts have been made to preserve the character of the original. RAF Marston Moor had a particularly attractive

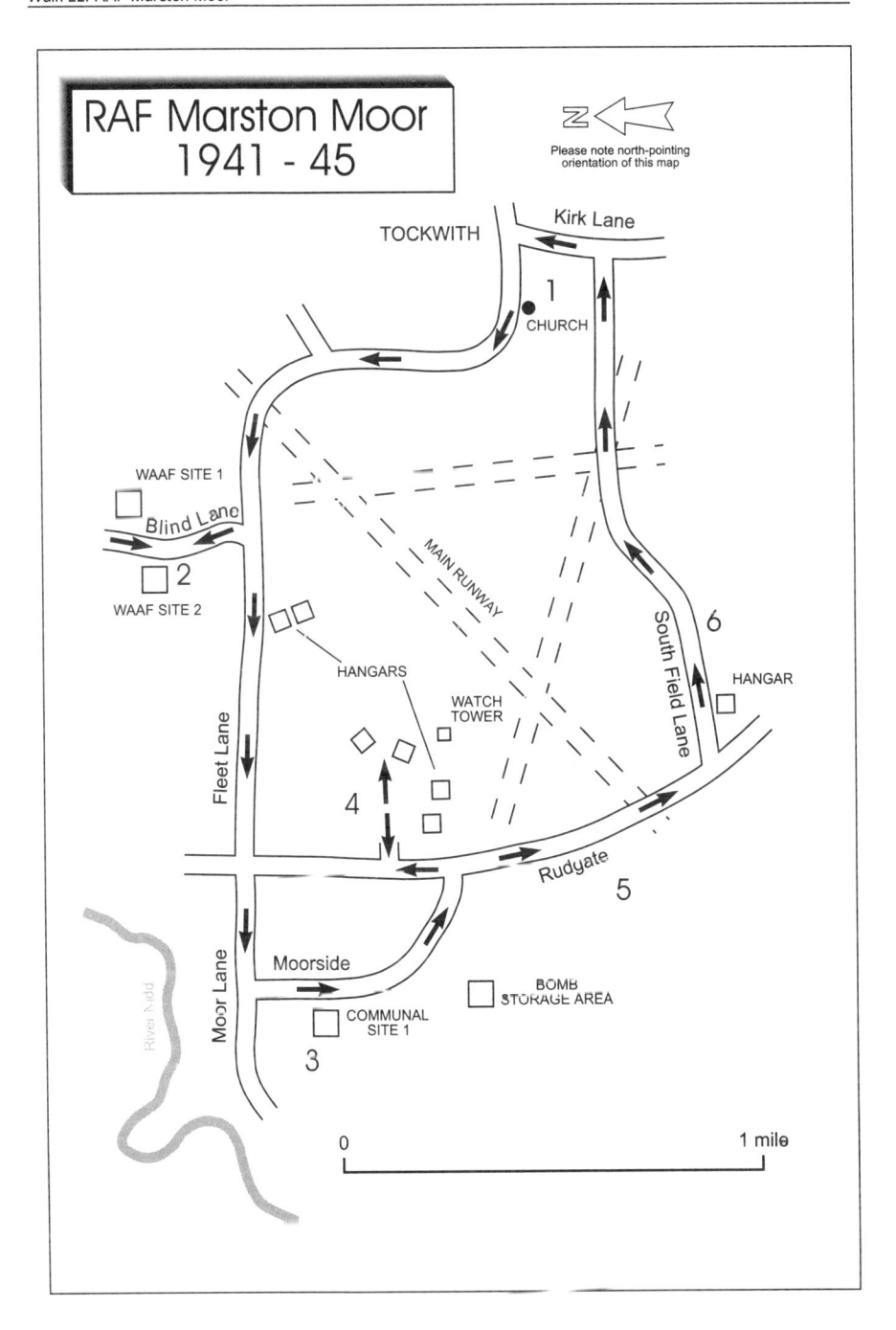

Walk 22: RAF Marston Moor

RAF Marston Moor 1941 - 45

N ←
Please note north-pointing orientation of this map

Kirk Lane

TOCKWITH

1 CHURCH

WAAF SITE 1

Blind Lane

2

WAAF SITE 2

MAIN RUNWAY

HANGARS

WATCH TOWER

Fleet Lane

South Field Lane

6

HANGAR

4

Rudyate

5

Moor Lane

Moorside

3 COMMUNAL SITE 1

BOMB STORAGE AREA

River Nidd

0 — 1 mile

entrance – and attractive it has remained, with a tree-lined curving road leading into the camp. The well-preserved guard house to the left of the entrance survives as the estate office.

5. Now retrace your steps along Rudgate. As you leave the main airfield site, a glance over to the left provides a good middle-distance view of the watch tower. On the right, the area occupied by the bomb stores comes into view. As might be expected, the concrete bunker-like structures are sufficiently durable to have survived. Further along Rudgate, to left and right are the remains of the main runway. Often, construction of an airfield would lead to the removal of roads and rights of way in a particular locality. At this point, Rudgate was obliterated, the land being requisitioned for the runway.

6. At South Field Lane, turn left to walk past another hangar – this time, a Type B1. The walk up South Field Lane is otherwise an uneventful one, punctuated only by the occasional sad pile of rubble. At the top of South Field Lane, turn left into Kirk Lane and back into Tockwith and your starting point.

Walk 23: RAF Acaster Malbis
1942-45

Route: Acaster Malbis – Airfield – Acaster Malbis

Starting Point: Mill Lane, Acaster Malbis

Length: 6 miles. Easy.

Map: Ordnance Survey Explorer 290

Access: Acaster Malbis lies to the south of York and is best approached via either the Copmanthorpe or Bishopthorpe junction of the A64 Leeds-Scarborough road. On road parking in the village.

About the Walk

The facilities of the Flying Training Schools, e established at the beginning of the Second World War, soon proved to be inadequate. Such bases had to cater not only for fresh pilots, but also for experienced pilots learning to fly an increasing number of new, improved aircraft rolling off the production line. To address the problem, the Relief Landing Ground (RLG) was introduced. As a rule, RLGs had no permanent buildings and only a single landing strip. In effect, they provided overflow facilities for the busier training schools and, as such, were sited as near as possible to their 'parent' stations. RAF Marston Moor had its own RLG, 5 miles (8 kilometres) to the south of York, adjacent to the village of Acaster Malbis.

The story of RAF Acaster Malbis is a strange one, not least of all because the station should never have existed. Although flat, the land is part of the marshy, mist-laden floodplain of the River Ouse – hardly conditions to facilitate take-off and landing. Yet, so desperate were the surveyors for sites that they recommended its development. The station opened on 6 January 1942 as a grass RLG for the Fighter Command base at nearby Church Fenton. Within a few weeks, the suitability of the site was brought into question with the death of the pilot of an American Airacobra fighter which crashed through the ice on the flooded banks of the Ouse.

Fighter Command moved out in March 1942 and, after a brief period with Flying Training Command – during which time further accidents occurred – the remarkable decision was taken to develop Acaster Malbis as a heavy bomber station. The contractors moved in and concrete runways were provided, together with two 'T2' hangars and dispersal sites with sufficient accommodation for 1394 servicemen and women. The site was handed over to Group 4 Bomber Command in 1943.

Group 4 clearly viewed their new station as a death trap and refused to send in any operational units. Towards the end of 1944, Acaster Malbis was transferred to Group 7 Bomber Command for training purposes and, at that stage, became an up-market RLG for RAF Marston Moor. The facilities were also used by a non-flying units – No 4 Aircrew School, and No 91 Maintenance Unit which utilised the site for bomb storage.

The station was closed on 28 February 1946 and the land returned to agricultural use. Although its contribution to the air war hardly merited the time and money invested in it, the airfield today is well preserved. Many buildings have survived in one form or another and, ironically, it constitutes one of the best remaining examples of a Second World War airfield.

Many buildings connected with Second World War airfields, although intended as temporary structures, survive to this day. Often adapted for farming use, they are unmarked on Ordnance Survey maps. The Picket Post for Site 10 Quarters, in the field opposite Woodside Farm (OS Explorer 290 5744) is one example.

The Walk

1. Begin in Acaster Malbis. Walk down the main street – Mill Lane – following the road round to the right to enter Intake Lane. To the left, as you walk down Intake Lane is the Caravan Village, located on what was Airfield Site No 11 – quarters for officers and sergeants and barracks for the men. Further along on the left is the Sewage Disposal Site.

2. Where Intake Lane turns sharply to the right, pause to view the buildings attached to Poplar Grove Farm on the left. These are the remains of Communal Site No 3. Continue to follow Intake Lane. In the small field before Beechlands Farm stood WAAF Communal Site No 2, now all but obliterated from the landscape. Only the ablutions building remains on the far side of the field. In the small rectangular field opposite Beechlands Farm stood Communal Site No 9. Again, one building survives – the Officers' Quarters.

3. Continue walking into Broad Lane. On the left, just before Brocket Wood, are the remains of WAAF Quarters Site No 8. Again, only one or two buildings survive. Turn left down the track – Green Lane – opposite Brocket Wood. To your right is Communal Site No 4. Some of the buildings have survived more or less intact, notably the Sergeants' Mess & NCO Sleeping Quarters block. To the rear of this site, adjoining Broad Lane, is Sick Quarters Site No 5. The Sick Quarters block itself together with the Ambulance Garage & Mortuary are well preserved.

4. Continue walking down Green Lane. On your right, the main airfield site is in view and accessible via a track to your left. This track links up with the minor road running between Acaster Malbis and Acaster Selby which was cut off to facilitate the construction of the airfield. Turn to the right and walk a little way down to the single surviving T2 Hangar, now used for warehousing. Immediately to the left of the hangar is the Watch Tower. This little gem – Type 343/43 – was an improvement on the early austerity design with its projecting balcony and external staircase, although the view was still comparatively poor.

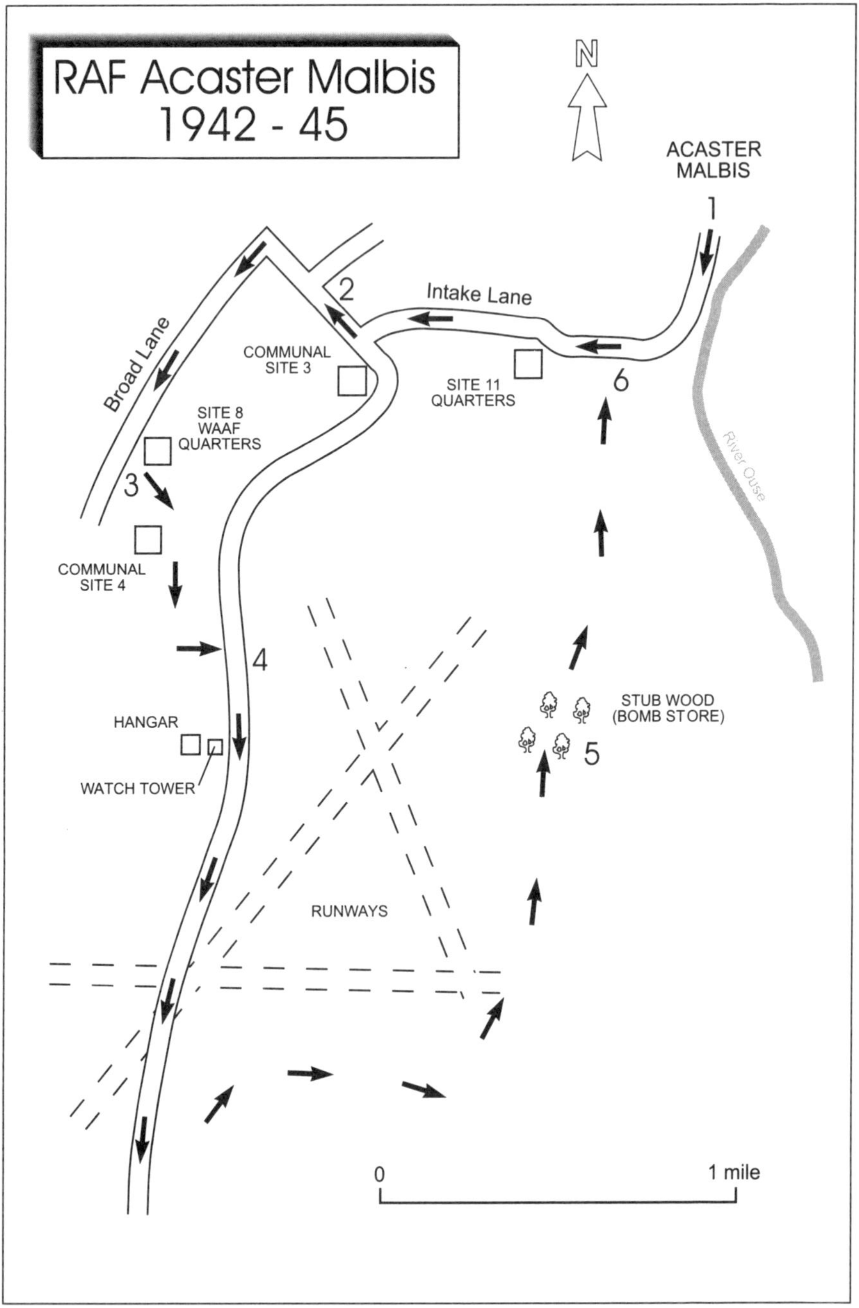
RAF Acaster Malbis
1942 - 45
N
ACASTER
MALBIS
1
2
Intake Lane
Broad Lane
COMMUNAL
SITE 3
SITE 11
QUARTERS
6
River Ouse
SITE 8
WAAF
QUARTERS
3
COMMUNAL
SITE 4
4
HANGAR
WATCH TOWER
STUB WOOD
(BOMB STORE)
5
RUNWAYS
0
1 mile

5. Turn back and walk back up the road to the point at which a public footpath – running round the perimeter of the main airfield site branches off to the right. Follow this path round to Stub Wood – pausing en route to view the main runway. Follow the path leading into the wood. Stub Wood is of interest because this was the Bomb Store Site.

6. Follow the path through the western edge of the wood and out into a field. The path runs in almost a straight line across three fields, emerging on Intake Lane, via the eastern rim of the Caravan Park. Turn to the right and follow Intake Lane back to your starting point in Acaster Malbis.

Also of Interest:

TEA SHOP WALKS IN THE YORKSHIRE DALES
Clive Price
Enjoy a stroll in the Yorkshire Dales rounded off with afternoon tea in a specially selected teashop. "A tantalising mixture of walks and eating places... a delightful concoction of exercise and culinary indulgence." £6.95

CURIOUS TALES OF OLD EAST YORKSHIRE
Howard Peach
Here is an entertaining guide to the history, folklore, traditions and social institutions of the Old East Riding, arranged in fourteen diverse chapters. Its scope is very wide-ranging, seriously researched and well illustrated bringing a heightened appreciation of the rich heritage of East Yorkshire. Foreword by David Davis, MP for Cottingham. £7.95

CURIOUS TALES OF OLD WEST YORKSHIRE
Marie Campbell
"A fascinating collection of odd tales ... curious clergymen, eccentrics and the allsorts of society's fringes." – NORTHERN EARTH 1999 "In this fascinating, entertaining, bustling...package of oddities, Marie Campbell ranges far and wide." BRADFORD TELEGRAPH & ARGUS £7.95

STRANGE WORLD OF THE BRONTËS
Marie Campbell
A comprehensive examination of new and little known material concerning the famous Brontë family and their involvement with occult practices. Essential reading for any serious Brontë student, including the Brontës occult connections. See the Brontës in a different light, their stranger/darker side; explore new material and fresh evidence about the Ripper case; digest new information about 'The Golden Dawn' – a Victorian occult group in Bradford; examine the Brontë birth charts. £8.95

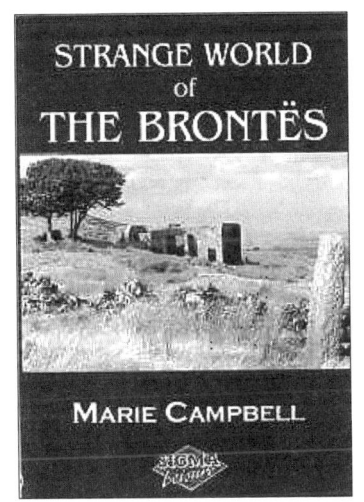

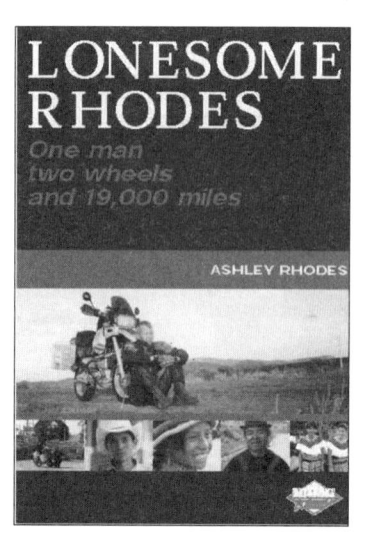

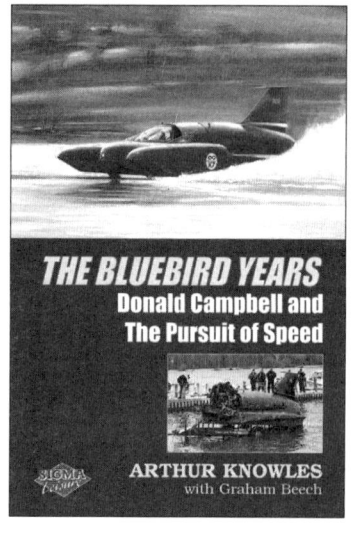

LONESOME RHODES – one man, two wheels & 19,000 miles
Ashley Rhodes

An outlandishly entertaining account of one of the world's most demanding journeys. There's humour, excitement, danger, human interest, geographical and historical detail, and big motor bikes – something for everyone. A first-hand account of what life on the road is like for a lone motorcyclist travelling the Americas. Includes a foreword by Bill Roache (well known as Ken Barlow of 'Coronation Street'). £8.95

COOK WITH CONFIDENCE
Beryl Tate

Forget the trendy TV chefs – Beryl Tate is a Cook with Confidence who skilfully applies her 35 years of catering experience to present more than 150 recipes. She includes valuable practical information in a style that is neither patronising to the novice, nor too rudimentary for the expert cook. Beryl not only describes how to cook, but also explains why her techniques work, and if you run into problems, provides many troubleshooting First Aid tips to get you out of sticky situations. So now you too can cook with confidence, satisfaction, and Yorkshire thrift. £7.95

THE BLUEBIRD YEARS: Donald Campbell and the Pursuit of Speed
Arthur Knowles with Graham Beech

Fully revised edition of the best-selling classic that documented Donald Campbell's attempts to raise the world water-speed record in his *Bluebird* jet-propelled boat to 300mph. Written by the man who was with Campbell throughout all the preparations and the final attempt that ended in tragedy. Features dramatic photographs, including shots of record attempts. Also includes complete coverage of the recovery of the wreckage of *Bluebird* and the funeral of Donald Campbell. £9.95

All of our books are available through booksellers. In case of difficulty, or for a free catalogue, please contact:
SIGMA LEISURE, 1 SOUTH OAK LANE, WILMSLOW, CHESHIRE SK9 6AR.
Phone: 01625-531035 Fax: 01625-536800. E-mail: info@sigmapress.co.uk
Web site: http//www.sigmapress.co.uk **MASTERCARD and VISA orders welcome.**